MW00474834

THE
7
CRUCIBLES

THE
7
CRUCIBLES

AN INSPIRATIONAL GAME PLAN

FOR

OVERCOMING ADVERSITY
IN YOUR LIFE

ALEC INGOLD

WILEY

For general information on our other products and services or for technical support, please contact our Customer Care Department within the United States at (800) 762-2974, outside the United States at (317) 572-3993 or fax (317) 572-4002.

Wiley publishes in a variety of print and electronic formats and by print-on-demand. Some material included with standard print versions of this book may not be included in e-books or in print-on-demand. If this book refers to media such as a CD or DVD that is not included in the version you purchased, you may download this material at http://booksupport.wiley.com. For more information about Wiley products, visit www.wiley.com.

Library of Congress Cataloging-in-Publication Data:

Names: Ingold, Alec, author.
Title: The 7 crucibles : an inspirational game plan for overcoming adversity in your life / Alec Ingold.
Description: Hoboken, New Jersey : Wiley, [2023] | Includes index.
Identifiers: LCCN 2022041522 (print) | LCCN 2022041523 (ebook) | ISBN 9781394171385 (cloth) | ISBN 9781394171392 (adobe pdf) | ISBN 9781394171408 (epub)
Subjects: LCSH: Resilience (Personality trait) | Success.
Classification: LCC BF698.35.R47 I54 2023 (print) | LCC BF698.35.R47 (ebook) | DDC 155.2/4—dc23/eng/20220914
LC record available at https://lccn.loc.gov/2022041522
LC ebook record available at https://lccn.loc.gov/2022041523

Cover Design: Paul McCarthy

SKY10040064_121622

Dedicated to all of the kids who are worried about being perfect. Chase greatness, not perfection. I pray you find purpose in this book and use it to bring that life to reality.

Contents

Preface

If you want to dare to be great, this book is for you. You're just like me.

If you've accepted a challenge in your life and made it a priority, you're on a journey full of ups and downs, wins and losses, peaks, valleys, and plateaus. You are chasing dreams that seem impossible to so many and inevitable to just a few friends and family. You want to be the 1% of the 1%, but you may not fully understand what it takes to get there.

I want to help you understand what it takes. I've been blessed beyond my wildest expectations in my journey to the National Football League. That journey was not easy, and as you'll read, it continues to challenge me on so many levels to this day.

The Seven Crucibles will take you inside how I combined my mental, physical, and most important, spiritual gifts to help me achieve my dream.

Whatever your dream is, I want you to live it, too. That's why I'm going to give you the answers to the tests of adversity I've faced along the way, especially when times seem the toughest. I hope you'll use what I'm going to tell you to chase those dreams, something every one of us needs to do. But the best part of *The Seven Crucibles* is it doesn't stop there. I want you to learn why adversity is essential to success. Chasing dreams without adversity attached diminishes those dreams because it means you're capable of chasing something even bigger!

Think of it this way. Chasing dreams without adversity is like winning a video game on the easiest setting. Dream BIG! Turn that difficulty meter up as high as it goes! Push yourself to your absolute limit, fall, get back up, and keep grinding.

I also want you to understand what happens on the other side of that dream. Have you ever asked yourself that question? Your life doesn't stop just because you accomplished what you want to. Life is a constant blur of motion, time, people and circumstances, and all of them can change in a matter of moments, like when you tear an anterior cruciate ligament, and you're faced with the possibility that you may never play another game in the NFL again.

How do you handle something like that? What do you do next?

When you chase your dreams and achieve them, of course you take some time to enjoy that your hard work paid off. But soon, you go through a necessary reality check.

In your dreams you only focus on the good, the light, the white. Nobody tells you that your dreams may come with nightmares. The failures, the fears, the dark. You have to respond to this realization with uncomfortable honesty. The longer you deny the dark, the harder it becomes to overcome that other side. That's part of the test of adversity that the crucibles in your life bring you. Ironically, it's also the part of life that nobody wants to face.

Nobody can choose how you respond or how quickly. This is an internal decision that I want to help you with. Understand that unless you face adversity, you'll never get to the other side of it and find all the gifts and rewards that were meant for you.

People often think they must confront the darkness on their own. That's absolutely not true. It's a process that nobody should do alone. Nor should you want to, especially if you have people and tools in your corner to help you.

That's why I wrote *The Seven Crucibles*. You will have few problems in the light, but it's the darkness that you must overcome to lead a happy and full life.

How you approach adversity in your life is a choice. I've been there and that's why I know I can help you. I want you to understand that adversity is inevitable, especially if you've set the bar high for your life. I want you to challenge yourself, and as odd as it may seem, I want you to fail from time to time.

That's because you'll learn resiliency from your failures. Failure will teach you how to adjust, and while it may not seem like it, put you one step closer to succeeding in whatever you decide you want to do with your life.

The Seven Crucibles is a journey for you, just like it has been for me to write it. But you aren't traveling toward a physical destination. As you read, I want you to think that you're traveling inward.

We're going to go through my toughest moments in life together, and in that way, I'll help you figure out the best ways to deal with your own pain and defeats.

I want you to want to own the darkness of your past. It's time to be honest with yourself and learn from all of those successes and failures. If you really want to see how great you can be, it's time to pick up this book and commit to facing your fears so that you will never again be afraid of failing. It's time to stop the self-sabotage and commit not only to yourself but to the people who count on you to be the best version of you.

Many books are written about how to succeed, but few talk about incorporating failures and adversity as part of that process. As you'll read, *The Seven Crucibles* is more than just about the setbacks I've encountered, it's also about the lessons I've learned despite those setbacks, on the way to being an NFL football player.

That's where we're going to relate: the failure. That's what nobody feels comfortable talking about. Everyone wants to show you their highlight reel. Highlight reels are great, but let's face it, they also don't reflect reality.

If you want to truly be the best version of yourself, you can't just own your highlight reel, you must be prepared to own everything: your good plays, your bad plays, your wins, and your losses. If you can do that, you have a chance at a truly great life.

So let's huddle up and see how great you really can be.

The Kickoff

My flesh and my heart may fail,
but God is the strength of my heart
and my portion forever.

Psalm 73:26

I'm not gonna lie, most people really don't care about special teams. None of the superstar players are on the field, fans don't pay much attention to what are considered routine plays to move the game along, and little more.

You might think these plays are a waste of time and interrupt the flow of the game, but for the men in the arena, the guys doing the dirty work that often goes unnoticed, this is where we make our living. We're a bunch of guys giving max effort at max velocity to chase one more pay day, or what the guys in the locker room refer to as a game check. Life as a special teams' player is pretty simple in one way. If we don't play, we don't get paid.

Remember the 2006 movie *Invincible* with Mark Wahlberg playing Philadelphia Eagles' player Vince Papale? Vince was pure grit and determination, finding any way to impact the game and make up for his lack of God-given ability. Punts and kicks have anywhere from 10 to 15 Vince Papales on the field during games these days. Every Vince has a burning reason to go full tilt every time he steps on the field.

Teams have these plays broken down to a science, as 22 guys start in a box, expand to 20 mph speeds over 50 yards, and condense into massive collisions in a matter of seconds.

That science makes special teams' plays routine almost every time.

Unfortunately, there was nothing routine for me about a punt play on November 14, 2021, late in the first quarter of the Las Vegas Raiders' game against the Kansas City Chiefs.

This was our national coming out party. We were 5-3 and we wanted to make a statement to a national audience that we were legit contenders. A chance to beat the big brother Chiefs that had our number since I'd been in the league.

I was dialed in. I was the Raiders' team captain and our team's National Football League Players Association rep in only my third year on the team. I had also been named a Walter Payton Man of the Year nominee and was a Pro Bowl alternate in 2019. I don't say this to pat myself on the back. I want you to understand how I play on special teams: typically, full tilt and all out. I always step onto the field with a sense of urgency and a need to relentlessly carve out a role for myself after going undrafted in 2019.

This was the week to let everyone know I was in the top tier of fullbacks in the world. My job wasn't always to rack up big stats. My job was to help our team find a way to "just win, baby" any way that I could. It was perfect for my brand of football, and I took pride in throwing key blocks, catching passes, barreling through people on handoffs, pumping up my teammates, and generating as much positive energy as I could on every play whether I was on the field or not.

I was also honored to be our special teams' captain, which is why I was on the field for that fourth down punt. On that play, our Pro Bowl punter, my guy A.J. Cole, sailed a punt to the Chiefs' Mike Hughes, who ran it back but fumbled on the play, giving us possession.

But I never saw the fumble.

I was lined up at right guard and my job was to get down field as quickly as possible to cover the punt. I got hemmed in at the line of scrimmage and was being blocked to the right. So, I planted my foot to turn left and accelerate to start my pursuit.

That's when it happened.

My leg gave out. My knee twisted. I heard a pop.

I knew immediately something was wrong. Really wrong. In a split second, I was on the ground grabbing my knee. My anterior cruciate ligament was shredded, completely torn.

And my season ended on that play.

I hobbled off the field and into the blue injury tent. After a quick look, the staff knew immediately what had happened.

Television footage from that day shows me being driven off the field in a cart, tears filling my eyes. You might assume those tears were because of the physical pain an injury like that can produce. But that's not why I was crying.

Truth be told, when you tear an ACL, there is very little physical pain.

If you were watching that day, the pain you saw was emotional pain.

I couldn't keep it in.

I had worked so hard, accomplished so many of my goals, and was living a dream I had spent my entire life working toward. I went from the highest of highs to a future filled with uncertainty in the blink of an eye.

When you're a pro athlete, or an athlete at any level, you accept injuries as part of the risk. I don't avoid contact or physicality. I pride myself on playing through injuries, bumps, and bruises . . . it's just a part of the game. You do what you can to guard against injuries, a meticulous routine that maximizes your chances at longevity in the league. Still, there aren't any guarantees.

Like so many other players before me, I found this out in the cruelest of ways.

As I write this, my injury took place a little over 12 weeks ago and I'm deep into a rehab process that will go on for several more months. Most ACL tears can't be sutured back together. To restore knee stability and repair the ACL, the ligament must be reconstructed. That's why the recovery process takes so long.

I've faced a lot of adversity in my life but never anything quite like this. I'm trying to use the time as productively as possible but I'm not gonna lie: some days (and many nights) are incredibly difficult, filled with anxiety, doubt, and fear.

If there is a silver lining, it's that this time has also given me a break to reflect on the adversities I've faced in my life. I've been able to put things into perspective, take a step back and think about what's important to me, and reconnect with my faith at an even deeper level.

I'm no stranger to adversity. I've overcome a lot in my life already. Using those experiences means I'm more prepared with what I need to do to overcome this torn ACL, which is arguably the biggest challenge I've ever faced.

Because I've always believed in giving back, I'm also using this time to share with you what I've learned about adversity along the way. Through my experiences, I want to help you to better overcome the various kinds of adversity you face in your life.

If I can unlock some of those answers for you, then the down time I've spent with my injury, no matter what comes next, will be time well spent.

What Are the Seven Crucibles?

A crucible is a situation of severe trial, or in which different elements interact, leading to the creation of something new. It's not just battling with something physically or mentally. A crucible is that problem that takes everything out of you, and tests you down to your core.

In other words, crucibles are the product of overcoming extreme adversity to produce change that results in something new, and often better.

The Seven Crucibles I want to tell you about—Purpose, Competition, Grindset, Support, Leadership, Discipline, and Perspective—have profoundly impacted my life. Each of them has been a form of severe trial, challenging me mentally, physically, spiritually, and emotionally. The "high temperatures" of these crucibles have transformed me and although the trials have been tough, these crucibles have made me a better person.

You might ask, "Are there more than seven crucibles?"

Of course, there are.

I'm positive you have a different amount or types of crucibles that have changed you.

For me, as a Christian with a profound commitment and connection to my faith, the number seven in the Bible represents completeness or perfection. Understand that in no way am I complete or perfect, but to this point in my life,

I have been put through these Seven Crucibles. Together, they have transformed me into the person I am today. In that way, I am the best possible, complete, and perfect version of who I am right now.

As I continue to grow, learn, and remain humbled by the world around me, there is little doubt that I'll add more crucibles. That's the whole point . . . that's life. Each of us conquers our crucibles, resulting in a deeper understanding of who we are, allowing us to use all those life lessons for our next inevitable test.

For now, I want to focus on these seven. I want to tell you how they have affected me, and share insights you can use in your own life. In this way, I hope to help you become a more complete and perfect version of who you are and were meant to be.

Overcoming adversity is also easier when it's a shared journey. Although our battles aren't the same, the notion of overcoming them is. As I tell you about my struggles, I know you'll see commonalities with your own struggles and take strength and comfort in knowing you and I and everyone else are connected by adversity.

The bottom line is this.

Do I have all the answers you're looking for? Not a chance.

Can I help you by sharing my struggles so that you can apply them in your own way? 100% yes.

As a pro football player, I've been blessed in many ways. You see one thing when my teammates and I step on the field every week. What you don't see is the daily sacrifice to get there. That's the job, that's where we relate the most, that's where the adversity happens. It's where the doubt, anxiety, and stress try to shake us the most.

I want you to understand that you've been blessed too. There's much more that binds us together than what separates us, no matter who you are or what you do in life.

Deciding to Embrace Change

Each of The Seven Crucibles teaches you something about the world, and something about yourself. While they are distinct, they also share one thing in common.

The Seven Crucibles are all about embracing change.

Change usually isn't pleasant. Many times, it's borne out of necessity, whether rehabbing from an ACL injury, getting over the loss of a loved one, forging new business relationships, or graduating from high school or college.

You can't live a great life and avoid change. The smartest thing you can do is embrace change. Change teaches you a lot about yourself. Change makes you tough and resilient.

Change is about learning how to overcome your doubts, anxieties, and fears about your future and letting go of the past. It's about figuring out what you're made of and what you really want in life, and what sacrifices you're willing to make if you really want to succeed. Change helps you assess your current state in life, and adjust it to get through the crucibles you've been blessed or challenged to endure.

As you'll read, I am supremely blessed with the life that God has bestowed upon me. Through my own crucibles, I've learned a lot about who I am and why God has brought change into my life.

Before I dig into The Seven Crucibles, I want to leave you with a story about what happened as I was sitting in the locker room after my injury took place.

Our quarterback, Derek Carr, came up to me, hugged me, and he said, "Deal with this however you need to deal with it for tonight. But when you wake up tomorrow, you gotta decide how you're going to come back from this. You're going to have to decide how you're going to attack this thing, and you're going to have to decide the mentality that you attack this rehab process you're facing."

My quarterback and my friend, a leader in every sense of the word, was telling me to embrace the change that was ahead of me.

I can't tell you how much his encouragement meant to me, especially coming from a man who's faced his own season-ending injury, and someone I've grown close to on an emotional and spiritual level.

For him to say that to me in what was one of the darkest moments of my life helped me realize that no matter what comes next, I'll be okay. I knew then that I wasn't going to waste time feeling sorry or bad about what happened. Instead, the next morning when I woke up, I decided how I was going to use this challenging crucible to my best advantage.

And then I began, in earnest, the long road back to a full recovery.

The Purpose
Crucible

A person's heart plans his way, but the
Lord determines his steps.

Proverbs 16:9

Every one of The Seven Crucibles is significant, but the Purpose Crucible might be the most important of all. Purpose is not just the root of what you do. It is who you are.

Your purpose determines what to focus on as you attack your goals. Purpose teaches you that how you attack one thing is how you attack everything. It's how you lead, compete, and implement discipline to succeed. Your purpose also frames your perspective. When you focus on your purpose and clearly define what it is, you give yourself a chance to win in the face of adversity.

Figuring out your purpose is tough, no doubt about it. Purpose requires figuring out what motivates and inspires you, how you want to fit into the world, and what the impacts are on your faith, among many others.

Purpose allows you to look closely at who you are, and the shortcomings or deepest fears you have in your life. For me, a big part of my purpose grew out of the fact that I was adopted. I was fortunate to join a kind, loving, and supportive family, but I was also aware from an early age that I was different. Being biracial, it wasn't a secret that nobody else in my family looked like me. That fed into a fear of failure, an irrational need to get external validation, and a hyper-driven goal of being a people pleaser.

Those things created a sense of loneliness, and never feeling like I was good enough. To overcome these fears, my purpose eventually morphed into working incredibly hard to make sure I never felt alone or that nobody would tell me they didn't want me.

I turned these insecurities inward and created a purpose to give me a sense of place and belonging.

Despite the success I've enjoyed, I still battle these types of things. When it's quiet and I have time to reflect, I can still go to some dark places. But I've also trained myself to recognize it when I do, and I'm now able to pull myself back to my purpose much quicker now.

Understand that your purpose is the sum total of your past, present, and what you want to do to create your best possible future. The transformation of a kid from Suamico, Wisconsin, to playing professional football meant facing my biggest fears before I could figure out my purpose in life.

Whether running your own business, being a great parent, or devoting your life to serving others, your worries and motivations will be different but just as important to you as mine are to me.

Our motivations are complex, and it takes a lot of courage to leap into uncertainty and discover your true purpose. Just like I did, you'll need to learn more about yourself and experience things that will drive you closer to that purpose or away from things that you aren't *truly* passionate about.

But there's more than that to finding your purpose. Due to the ongoing nature of life and the changes you go through, your purpose isn't necessarily a stationary target. Your purpose is dynamic.

Here's the best example I have and one that took place just a short while ago.

I've given everything I have to the Las Vegas Raiders for the past three seasons. Blood, sweat, tears, passion, drive, and total commitment to the team. I held nothing back. It's the way I approach everything.

I was looking forward to recovering 100% from my ACL injury and remaining an essential part of the Raiders organization for many seasons to come. And then, I was called into the general manager's office one day and told that even if I was completely healthy, they didn't know if I'd be a fit for the team anymore.

I was crushed, filled with intense feelings of sadness, confusion, unfairness, and betrayal. I discounted the business side of the decision, but in the end, that's what pro football is.

It took a couple of days, but I set my feelings aside and recalibrated my purpose. I focused on myself and what I could offer, for the Raiders or somewhere else in the NFL. And in an instant, in the face of adversity, my purpose shifted. Instead of making it my purpose to play for the Raiders, I locked in on a new purpose focused on a new journey and a mountain I'd have to climb.

Like all the other crucibles you'll read about, the Purpose Crucible is a living, breathing challenge that requires you to react to what life throws at you. When you understand this, your mindset shifts from seeking external validation to finding an internal motivation that drives your purpose in life.

When you make this shift, you genuinely control who you are, and you accept the circumstances you've been dealt for what they are and nothing else. You accept your imperfections, find greater peace, and can more easily shift to a purpose you are now meant to pursue. During these times, when you're redefining your purpose, all the other crucibles you'll read about come into play.

The beauty of thinking this way is that I already know the result. As I write this, I don't know where I'll go next, what team I'll play for, or what kind of contract I'll land.

But I do know that one of my ongoing purposes is to inspire belief. To that end I'll combine all my talents, skills, abilities, grit, and determination, and thrive through this temporary adversity. With the right purpose-driven mindset, I can still be an inspiration to others and give them a blueprint to chase their own greatness.

Identity and Purpose Are Not the Same

Do you know what your "why" is?

Have you thought about why you're living your life the way you do now? Why do you do what you do? When was the last time you thought about your purpose in life?

If there's a silver lining to my ACL injury, it gave me time to think about who I am and what I'm supposed to be doing with my life.

I've realized that my identity as a professional football player is not necessarily the same as my purpose in life. The two can work together, but my purpose is bigger and more overarching than my identity.

Identity is who I am. When I go into a doctor's office or the Department of Motor Vehicles and fill out paperwork, I am revealing to the world what my identity is.

My purpose, in part, is fueled by my identity. While identity is the WHO in my life, purpose is the WHAT and WHY.

Because I've enjoyed success in my identity as a professional football player, I'm able to use that spotlight to propel my purpose forward, which is to inspire others and help them believe that they can be the best versions of themselves.

The adversity of my injury has allowed me to sharpen that focus and think about what changes I can make so that my purpose extends beyond my playing days. That's how I'm using my current identity as a rehabbing football player to extend and feed into my lifelong purpose.

Let me say that again, my identity is who I am right now. My purpose is what I do throughout my life as well as the reason why.

Other people and circumstances are things you can't control, and do have an impact on your identity. But the power of purpose is that only YOU can define why you do what you do.

Identity changes more often than purpose does. Over the years, I'll go from playing football at a college and pro level to retiring and assuming a new identity. My purpose will remain intact, but it will also be shaped by the events, people, and challenges I faced along the way.

Think about your identity and purpose and how they serve you. Do they align with each other? Do both energize you? Can you anticipate crossroads in your life where these things will change? Are you ready for unforeseen events, such as an ACL injury, that will impact both your identity and purpose?

Sooner or later, you'll face crucibles in your life. Understand that God has blessed you with specific skills and abilities that give you gifts to enjoy doing what you love and feed into your identity and purpose.

When your identity and purpose are challenged, you get the opportunity to go through this crucible with a smile on your face and love in your heart, listening for the lessons you need to hear so you can chase the best version of yourself. If you create this kind of mindset, you'll be able to share your joy and positivity with others in the spirit of gratitude.

Paying it forward with gratitude costs nothing, but creates extreme value when you connect with family members, friends, fans, or even during chance encounters with strangers.

Because I understand how my identity and my purpose work together, I can fight through all the aches, pains, bruises, time demands, and mental hurdles it takes to play in the NFL. Trust me, there are a lot of them, and they aren't always easy to overcome.

The funny part is when your identity and your purpose are linked together, what others see as sacrifices don't seem like sacrifices to you. You can transform negatives into positives effortlessly. You have no problem getting up at 6 a.m. to do some rehab, whether it's for broken ribs, a sprained ankle, or a torn ACL. You're motivated to put the work in because you truly believe in what you're doing. It's bigger than you. The back of your head, where purpose resides, fuels you to relentlessly chase away all obstacles in your way.

In short, when your identity and your purpose are aligned, all things are possible.

The Oracle Revelation

After my junior year in college, I got benched. While I saw it as only a temporary blip, my support system (also often referred to as my parents), thought it might be a good idea to start thinking about a backup plan if football didn't pan out.

At the time, I wasn't thrilled with their suggestion, but like most parent's advice to children at that age, they were probably right. Shortly after that, I put on a suit and tie and went to a job fair at the Kohl Center on the University of Wisconsin–Madison campus.

I didn't have any experience attending job fairs, but I was a personal finance major, so I talked to a lot of banks and financial institutions, trying to figure out where I might fit as a financial advisor, a certified financial planner, or a certified public accountant. At the time, the big buzz for finance majors was trying to land a job with a software technology company.

And that's when I came across this company called Oracle. You may laugh at this, but I had no idea what Oracle was. I'd never heard of it before. I saw a long line of students waiting to talk to its reps, so I figured they were worth investigating. While waiting my turn, I Googled the company and found out it was heavy into software. If you're young and ambitious, selling tech software means money, lots of money. Like everyone else in line, that got my attention.

I fired up my competitive side and had a great initial meeting with the reps. I signed up for a callback, and then I went home and did my homework on them. A week later, an Oracle recruiter called me for a quick phone interview. I thought I did okay, and there was some promise of taking it to the next level with the company based on what the recruiter told me. At that point, I dug in and did deep research on not only Oracle, but what it would be like to get into tech sales as a career.

Armed with this info, I crushed the following interview . . . hit it out of the park! The interviewer told me he needed to introduce me to his boss who would be in town a few weeks later. He thought I'd be a perfect fit for Oracle, and he was sure his boss would think so, too.

I expected to be a part of a small group of people advancing to the next round of interviews, maybe a pool of five or ten people. It was an in-person interview on campus, and when I opened the door to where the interviews were taking place, I was greeted by about 100 people suited up with résumés in hand just like me, sitting in the lobby.

Oh, boy, I didn't expect that.

But I had done my research, had two great phone interviews, put together a killer résumé and cover letter, and had my competitive game face going for me. It took me a moment, but I was ready to win!

Then this happened.

I had my interview, and before I left that office, the interviewer told me not to worry about everyone waiting in the lobby, and he offered me a job on the spot.

He said, "I love how you handle yourself. You're confident, well-spoken, articulate, intelligent, and motivated. The fact that you're a student-athlete means you also know how to compete and win. That's the kind of person we're looking for here at Oracle. Go tell your parents you got a job with us and celebrate. Congratulations!"

I didn't expect that either.

I hopped into my rusted out 2005 Nissan Pathfinder and cranked up "Dreams and Nightmares" by Meek Mill. The bass was bumping, the mirrors were rattling, and I was going nuts all the way back to my apartment. I couldn't wait to celebrate with my roommates. Just one problem . . . it was the middle of the day on Wednesday, and both were in class! So,

I tried to call my dad, but he was tied up in meetings. Then I called my mom, but she was still teaching.

Things might have turned out differently if any of them had picked up the phone.

Left all alone, I started thinking.

Did I want to sell software for longer than I could imagine? Could I find passion and purpose going on sales calls and sitting in an office at this stage in my life?

You already know what the answer was.

While I should have been completely excited about working for Oracle, the honest answer is that I was not. I had another year of playing Big Ten football in front of me, and I came to Wisconsin to play!

As odd as it sounds, the Oracle offer was a nice piece of adversity to have. And I view it as adversity because it forced me to think long and hard about my true purpose in life. I was confronted with the challenge of making an important decision.

That day, alone in my apartment, I took off my coat and tie, splashed some cold water on my face, and gave thanks for the opportunity that had come my way.

Then I turned down the offer to work for Oracle.

At that point in my life, my identity was completely wrapped up in being a football player for Wisconsin. My purpose was to use that platform to inspire my teammates to join me in balling out, giving everything we had every day we stepped on that field.

It took a great opportunity, albeit the wrong opportunity, to realize my purpose. I rededicated myself to being the best player I could now that all doubts had been removed.

After resolving the challenges of the Purpose Crucible, I moved forward, and I've never looked back at my purpose since that time.

• • •

Here are some things for you to consider as you confront your own Purpose Crucible.

- How well do you handle change and rejection? What do you feel when your worth is challenged?
- How do you fortify your thoughts and protect your current identity and long-term purpose in life?
- For me, a big part of defining my purpose is calling upon my faith. Falling in love with the process and becoming more Godlike every day is part of the plan, too.
- Have you had opportunities like I had with Oracle, only to realize as amazing as they are, that deep down they weren't right for you?

Until you figure it out, your purpose is a crucible you'll need to confront at some point if you ever want to be happy in life.

Pray, meditate, talk to people you trust, and listen to your gut. You must work at this and do whatever it takes. When you do, your purpose will crystalize and become clear, leading you to peace and clarity in your life.

The Competition Crucible

Do nothing out of selfish ambition or vain conceit.
Rather, in humility value others above yourselves,
not looking to your own interests, but each of you
to the interests of the others.

Philippians 2:3–4

You're going to need to do some reflection before continuing with this crucible. If you don't want to be tested, if you don't want to truly commit with all the energy you have, if you aren't willing to have an altercation in your life . . . put down the book right now. This isn't for you.

You can't be the best version of yourself without an altercation. Not a confrontation, an altercation. What do I mean by that?

Competition is often seen as a battle, a fight. Iron sharpens iron right? One piece of iron doesn't get sharper by confronting another piece of iron. Nothing happens when the two pieces of iron are brought together. They must be hit together, creating friction and sparks. This takes effort, energy, and aggression, over and over again to turn a piece of iron into its sharpest form. Just as iron versus iron requires an altercation, you must also embrace altercations physically and emotionally to overcome competitive adversity in your life.

Even if you're not an athlete, you're constantly competing at something if you're in any type of game. Whether in business, school, with yourself, or others, you compete countless times a day.

The question you need to ask yourself isn't "Do I compete?" but "How do I compete?"

Competition is born out of adversity. To navigate the Competition Crucible, you need to start by understanding the proper way to compete.

The Right Way versus the Wrong Way

Welcoming competition into your life should excite you, not threaten you. To compete the right way, the first thing you need to do is frame competition as a chance to achieve a higher degree of excellence in yourself. Embrace the challenge, and you will start to breed excellence in all that you do.

When pressure mounts because you're being challenged mentally and physically, understand that you can control your preparation, not your performance. When you're preparing, you can truly test your limits. That's where you force yourself to be uncomfortable, to stress yourself more than you've ever been stressed.

You can have all the effort, intentionality, and consistency in the world to put yourself in a position to succeed and still fall short. Embracing this reality, and not fighting it is the first step in competing.

Remember, the enemy gets a vote too. In some cases, the player or the team you're up against may just be better than you or your team on a given day, despite your absolute best efforts. You might hear me say, "The enemy gets a vote, too" if I had to block all-world linebacker Ray Lewis. I can do everything right, but he still gets a say, as he did with most people he went up against. Circumstances just happen in life; doesn't mean you should stop giving 100% genuine effort and energy.

It's not easy to get over this hump for some people. Competition is a daily fight when you're a fullback in the

NFL. I'm under a lot of pressure every day to compete, partly because you can't live for very long on past glories. You're often judged by how well you played over the course of your last season, your last game, and sometimes, your last down. The stakes are high, and that creates a cutthroat environment.

Unfortunately, that can lead to behaviors that are the wrong way to compete.

I've heard horror stories of veterans not telling rookies what to do or how to do things on and off the field, sabotaging their growth so that the veteran can keep his job for one more season. Thankfully, that's never happened to me. But it exists. I've heard about it, and I've seen it more often than I admit. It's an extra layer of adversity added to a job that's already incredibly difficult to do at such a high level.

When you're part of the same team, there is a better way to compete, a right way to compete.

I always approach competition with my teammates by trying to find a way that makes everyone better for the team's overall good. I practice hard because that's a form of competition that makes my teammates better. I compete hard on every play in every game and try to set an example that raises the competitive spirit for everyone in the game and on the sidelines.

I genuinely care about the well-being of the guys I'm with, and I hope they respect me enough to want the best for me and care enough to push me as hard as I push them. When this is part of your team's culture, you create a healthy place where everyone's goals are aligned for the good of the team.

If you're squared up against me, maybe as another fullback, or on special teams, or a linebacker on a run fit, I'm going to come at you with a big smile on my face and try to knock you on your ass, strictly with the goal of making you a better player. I dare you to get the best of me. To beat me. To try and knock me on my ass as well. Going full speed and full throttle.

Here's why. When I do that for you, I'm making myself a better player, too. It also means I respect you. I care about you to make you the best version of yourself while also making me the best version of myself.

If you win a battle against me at the end of the day, iron has sharpened iron, and both of us have won.

That's the right way to compete.

Although football provides countless opportunities to compete against teammates and opposing players, the place where I learned the most about overcoming adversity and competing the right way took place on a padded mat and not on a grassy field.

The Kazik Lesson

I played a lot of football in high school, but I took my first steps on a wrestling mat.

The competitive part of wrestling is a lot different than football. As a team sport, there are places you can hide from time to time if your results and effort aren't what they should be. Wrestling puts you on an island.

It's you versus the man across from you. The better man gets his arm raised, and the loser shakes hands and walks off the mat. There is no place to hide if you don't win your match.

My dad was a wrestling coach, so I started wrestling when I was four years old. I maximized that "insiders' advantage." By the time I was a junior in high school, I was a favorite to run through the season and finish with a state title.

Although we had a great program at Bay Port High School, there wasn't always a diverse selection of competition at the 220-pound weight class. I couldn't get better if there was no iron to sharpen iron.

Enter Andy Kazik.

Kazik was a beast. My wrestling coaches brought him in as an assistant coach and my practice partner. He was also a former NCAA Division III national champion from Lawrence University, famous for his grueling workout sessions.

With Kazik on board, I immediately competed against him the wrong way.

I avoided him for the first month he was around.

When we did go toe to toe, he beat me up in practice every day. I didn't realize it at first, but he was making me mentally tougher as he was making me a physically better wrestler too.

He did that by taking me down in the first 30 seconds of our practices. It was humbling, and I didn't particularly like it. But I finally realized what he was doing was preparing me for those times I might get taken down in the state tournament.

His lesson was simple but highly effective. He taught me not to worry about early takedowns because I was getting taken down by him every day in practice, and I was learning not only what it felt like to get taken down but what it felt like to get back up again and compete even harder.

Kazik knew the importance of being uncomfortable in the practice room. He knew that being uncomfortable isn't a choice . . . it's inevitable. The only choice you have is WHERE you experience that discomfort. If you truly commit and put yourself in uncomfortable situations in the practice room, you allow yourself to shine when the lights are on. In this phase of my life, I hated being uncomfortable, and avoided it as much as possible.

In the end, Kazik taught me about killer instinct. I crushed the competition for the rest of my junior year but when I was put in an uncomfortable situation in the state tournament, I choked.

I thought I had all the pieces to go all the way, but I needed to go through more adversity before developing the killer instinct, like a shark that smells blood in the water, before reaching my goal. That season came to an underwhelming end with only a state qualification and 2nd Team All-Conference recognition.

I had unfinished business on the mat, but I also had an offer to play football at the University of Wisconsin-Madison campus going into my senior year. The big hurdle I had to overcome was whether to wrestle in my senior year with that scholarship offer on the table. It was never really an issue for me, even at the risk of getting injured.

I knew from the start I was going to compete. I had something left to prove to myself.

Kazik worked me hard my senior year, and I started reeling off a string of victories despite juggling practices between the two sports and missing days here and there because I was on official college visits.

Kazik, my dad, and my coaches gave me higher levels of confidence than ever before. It was fueled by the fact that I was in the best shape of my life, never worrying about having to take extra steps to cut down to weight for upcoming matches. Between the two sports, I was already doing it.

Late in the season, I got the final boost I needed. Kazik and I were practicing, going at it hard, and for the first time in over a year, I took him down. I put him on the mat!

That may not sound like a big deal, but it was a graduation day for me. Kazik was a black belt in Brazilian jiu jitsu, a national championship wrestler, and a full-grown man . . . and I legitimately took him down.

From what I remember, it didn't go over all that well with Kazik.

And it didn't help that I was a little cocky about it as well. I thought, "Sick, I just took down freaking Kazik!" His train of thought was different from mine. This man controlled everything about our practices for the longest time, and instead of telling me, "Good job, Alec," he pressed and intensified the practice. We went forehead to forehead. You could sense an immediate change as we went right back at it.

My glory was short-lived.

He dominated me in the worst (best?) possible way for the rest of that practice. It was a wrestling ass whooping. We went blow for blow until I couldn't hang anymore. I was physically exhausted and mentally broken. My arms couldn't move, sweat and blood were pouring down my face. It got to the point where I couldn't get up and I couldn't stand on my feet. Nothing was working the way it was supposed to. It was a grown man altercation.

I thought I had scored a great victory that day. Instead, I cracked up and broke down in the locker room. I was drenched in sweat. I had reached my limit. I was an emotional mess. I had reached the end of my competitive rope. I emptied my locker and quit. I didn't need this anymore. I was going Division 1, man. What the hell am I doing getting my ass kicked and embarrassed like this for?

I didn't realize it at the time, but that was the best thing for me, and here's why.

I was competing in the safe space of practices. My mental and physical toughness reached new levels that I'd never experienced before. That horrible, exhausted feeling was actually producing growth in me. Growth I'd need to achieve next-level results. And that's precisely what I did.

That night I was forced to make a decision. To truly commit. To sacrifice more than I ever have to accomplish something I've fallen short of too many times. When I woke up the next morning, I brought all my wrestling gear back to the high school, and I dominated.

I didn't just win; I dominated.

As a senior at Bay Port, I went 41-0 and won the Wisconsin State Wrestling Division 1 WIAA state title in the 220-pound division.

I competed hard in every one of those matches. But it was the competition behind the scenes with Andy Kazik that made all the difference in winning and losing that season.

The Lesson Carries Over

Learning the right way to compete in high school carried over into college football and the NFL. I would need to tap into those lessons as a member of the Raiders when I got into the biggest competition of my life.

As an undrafted free agent in my rookie year, I came into camp and had to compete for a job against Keith Smith, a five-year veteran who was above me in the team depth chart. I was equally excited as a rookie and fearful at how different the environment was from college to the pros. In college, you're often in the spotlight as a star on your team. As an NFL rookie, you're just one of the many guys on the team where everyone was a star at one time or another. That takes some getting used to.

Fortunately for me, Keith understood the value of competing the right way by helping his teammates. He taught me a lot about becoming a professional football player and how to pay it forward, even as we competed against each other. He made all the difference in the world as I transitioned from college to the pros.

Sadly, Keith suffered a knee injury at the beginning of training camp, and I moved up and over him in the Raiders' depth chart. He was released a short time later. Although our time together was brief, I learned a lot from him about competing the right way at the NFL level.

Fast forward a few years later, when I tore my ACL.

To fill the hole created by my injury, the team added Sutton Smith to the 53-man roster. Although I was traumatized by my season-ending injury, I had to put that behind me and keep competing. I flashed back to the valuable lessons Kazik and Keith had taught me.

Sutton didn't have much experience as a fullback, so my mission was clear from the jump. For the good of the team, I wanted him to be the best possible fullback so that our offense could thrive, and the Raiders would do well. I started working with him to download and refine his skills in every way I could. We worked on handling the demands of the position, and the mental toughness he would need to succeed.

Helping Sutton wasn't an issue for me, although some people will see it as me helping a guy who could ultimately take my job. That's a selfish way of approaching football, and even more important, a selfish way of approaching life.

Don't ever let your insecurities become your enemies.

Instead, I view things as if you work with someone to make them a better competitor, then their successes are reflected upon you, and they become your successes too.

The important takeaway is this. Learn how to compete the right way. Embrace competition if you ever hope to win at anything significant in your life. Make the right way to compete such an ingrained habit that it is the only way you know as you go about living your life.

Also, understand that competition is about supporting your teammates, even when you're going head-to-head with them. Give freely and watch how it comes back to you many times over.

When you win those battles, you win honestly. You can still hold your head up high when you lose, knowing that the competition made you, the guy across from you, and your entire team better.

• • •

How do you approach competition?

- Are you threatened by it or do you view it as an opportunity to see iron sharpen iron? If you're part of the same team, do you have enough character to appreciate that everyone has the same common goal of trying to win at whatever the team's goal is?

- Do you have an Andy Kazik in your life? If not, would you welcome somebody like that? Someone who would care enough and push you hard enough to drive you to your best version of you?
- Can you put your personal goals aside for a higher purpose, knowing that when one part of a team is elevated, the entire team is elevated? Can you be a Keith Smith type of person, or like me a few seasons later, helping Sutton Smith as part of the right way to compete?

The Competition Crucible seems easy to master at first. But when you dig deeper, you'll see that the quality of your character is often defined by the quality of how you compete.

That's the best way to overcome competitive adversity.

The Grindset
Crucible

But the one who does not know and does things deserving punishment will be beaten with few blows. From everyone who has been given much, much will be demanded; and from the one who has been entrusted with much, much more will be asked.

Luke 12:48

You probably haven't heard the word *Grindset* before.

No worries, because *Grindset* is a word I made up to describe the next step you're willing to take on your journey to greatness.

Your Grindset is defined by your character. It's having an alignment of your heart, mind, and body all moving toward that singular goal or achievement. It's also having supreme ownership of your previous trials and tribulations, all of your wins and all of your losses.

You can write down a goal, and you can probably chase it for a decent amount of time. But what happens when you forget why you started this journey in the first place? What happens when talent isn't enough to keep you moving forward?

You can picture this as someone climbing a mountain. The top of the mountain is a goal you write down and you're ready to chase. As you approach the base of the mountain to start your climb, you need to have a moment where you take accountability and responsibility for this climb you're about to undergo. You are at point A, and point B is a mountaintop away from you. Grindset is about taking supreme ownership of where you're at right now and what you're willing to go through to get to where you want to be.

After that conscious decision, it's time to climb. At the beginning of the climb, you'll have a lot of energy, which is great! Use it. When you climb as effectively and efficiently as possible starting out, you'll cover quite a bit of ground.

There's going to be a point where you need to take a break. You might be sore, self-doubt may start to creep in, and if you can't see the top, you'll wonder how far you've made it up the mountain. It's easy to look down and see you've traveled quite a ways from the base. You may even give yourself an "attaboy" to pump you up. But when you look up you see how much farther you have to go, you might also get discouraged to find out it's much farther than you expected.

It's okay to take a peek at the peak, but you must also remind yourself that you started this climb for a reason. When you fixate on the peak, you lose focus on the very next step right in front of you. The climb becomes grueling, exhausting, and challenging.

It's at this moment that you need to lock back into your Grindset. Align your mindset and heartset to continue on and take one step at a time.

There will be mental and physical challenges in any mountain you climb. There will be adversity. Plan for it. Expect it. Embrace the suck.

Remember why you started your journey. Literally carve out time to stop and think about it. Fall in love with climbing the mountain, not what the view from the peak looks like. With this focus and determination, you'll be able to accomplish the goal you set, and you'll be able to say that you did it.

Here's the other thing to understand. That momentary feeling of success and accomplishment is fleeting, and all of a sudden, you're going to look up and there's a whole new mountain to climb.

If you focus on the peak, and the view from where you're at, this will be extremely discouraging. You might quit, or just stay right where you're at . . . it's comfortable there! Some people settle for living on small hills, and for them, that's okay.

But if you fall in love with the climb, if you truly want to see how great you can be, if your Grindset is aligned, you'll undoubtedly climb again.

The Grindset's Two Brothers . . . Mindset and Heartset

To embrace your Grindset, you need to lock in on two ingredients that go into a Grindset mentality. Those two things are mindset and heartset.

Your mindset is how you think and talk to yourself. Mindset is extremely powerful in focusing your internal energy toward positivity or negativity. On your journey there are going to be several external circumstances you can't control. This should be expected, not feared. How you react to those things is something you can control.

With a correct mindset, you'll find positive elements in all the adversity thrown your way. Your ability to mentally deal with all the crap life throws at you is a skill that's also a daily fight, but it's a fight worth having. Staying positive and communicating to yourself in a positive manner is essential in continuing your journey to the best version of yourself.

If you can dial in the correct mindset and be consistent with it, you'll make bad days average and average days good. Good days will become great days! That small shift in perspective can really compound results time and time again.

Your heartset is the energy and passion behind your journey. If something is true to you, and true to your heart, that is empowering. Your heartset is an ability to find energy in the depths of despair. When you don't know how you're possibly going to make it to the top of your mountain, your heartset keeps one foot moving in front of the other.

You've heard the phrase, "He's got a lot of heart to take this on," or "She gave it her heartfelt best." It's hard to explain other than heartset is another level of determination, energy, and the "it" factor that turns underdogs into winners.

Like mindset, heartset is also a conscious decision. Nobody can make you tap into these two brothers of Grindset. Either you do, and make them work to your fullest advantage, or you don't, and then you make the struggle to achieve your goals that much harder.

Talent Is Overrated

Talent is overrated.

You're probably wondering where I'm going with this. But it's the truth.

And here's why.

Every player in the NFL is extremely talented. You can't make it to this level without working your tail off to hone your craft. You work on getting faster, stronger, jumping higher, and on dozens of other small skills that make you an athletically gifted football player.

In that way, almost all players are equal. However, here's what I've discovered.

Talent is a floor.

Your character determines your ceiling.

Talent gets the lion's share of the attention but if you don't combine critical character traits with that talent, you'll never reach your full potential. I've applied that to my football career, but you can also apply it to whatever challenges or goals you've set for yourself in life.

Character traits are a series of small pieces of a puzzle that, when assembled, feed heavily into your talent. The question then becomes: "What character traits should you aspire to in pursuit of your goals?"

I want to share with you some traits I think are the most valuable and have worked best for me.

Your list will probably be different from mine, and that's okay. The goal here is to define and then relentlessly chase the best version of you.

Look in the Mirror

My old running back coach with the Las Vegas Raiders, Kirby Wilson, gave us a mirror when our team was on a losing skid. His message to us was simple.

"The first person you should point a finger at when times get tough is the person you see in this mirror. When times get tough, accept everything you've done to this point and look in the mirror to fix what's wrong before you look anywhere else in this locker room."

Being accountable starts with you. It's up to you to reflect and accept where you're at in life.

Take supreme ownership—all of the good parts and the bad. When you do this, you lay the groundwork for making your life better. If you can't do this, you're hurting yourself, your teammates, and everyone else around you.

It's not easy. When I tore my anterior cruciate ligament, I wanted to blame the coaches, Kansas City Chiefs' players, and even the grass before reflecting and accepting that maybe I put myself in a bad position to try and make a play. Only after I looked in the mirror did I begin to heal.

Align Yourself with Like-Minded Teammates

When I was in school at the University of Wisconsin, I had a football coach tell us a story of Belgian plow horses. One Belgian plow horse alone can pull over 8,000 pounds. When you put another plow horse right next to the original one, they can pull over 22,000 pounds . . . way more than just double the original amount.

Even more remarkable is what happens when these two plow horses get to know each other and train together. Two Belgian plow horses that live and train together can pull up to 32,000 pounds, four times as much as the original weight. The team that these two create is much greater in value than just the sum of their parts.

Your Grindset, mindset, and heartset becomes greater than the sum of their parts when you assemble them together. You create alignment with the right kind of self-talk and your outward demeanor as a teammate, parent, husband, business owner, and in every other part of your life. Alignment makes the grind easier. Alignment lets you create habits that feed into your talent. Alignment creates passion. And as I've discovered in the NFL, passion wins out many times over more talented teams.

This character trait is what made it a lot easier for me to face a nine-month rehab process, with no guarantee that I could play again at 100%. Alignment is why I'm willing to give it everything I've got, make sacrifices, exorcize doubt and negativity, and get my entire being leaning into what I really want, which is to play football at the highest level again.

Find a Grit Factory

My time in college had its fair share of ups and downs. Nothing was handed to us at UW. You earned your playing time just like you earned your grades in class and your respect in the locker room. There's a tradition of taking your lumps and learning your lessons. Whether you're a walk-on or a five-star recruit, there's an expectation of developing and learning what it takes to be a smart, tough, dependable student athlete. There are no shortcuts, and that's why it's recently been dubbed the Grit Factory.

The Grit Factory is all about respecting yourself and understanding if you want anything worthwhile in life, you must spend long, hard hours putting in the work.

Trust me when I say this. The people you're competing against all spend huge blocks of time in a Grit Factory. One of you is going to spend more time there than the other, and I think you already know who has the best chance of winning. Put in the time.

The Grit Factory is a place where no shortcuts are allowed. It is a place where stubbornness is welcome and sacrifice is expected. It can also be a lonely place. When you tear your

ACL, there will be many days where you'll go into the training facility, and nobody will be at the training tables except you. You know you've got to dig down deep and try to get better for the next two solitary hours, even when you can barely straighten your leg.

No One Cares

One night during my ACL recovery, I was going through it. I couldn't sleep. I was emotionally drained, questioning my future and everything that was going on in my life. I ended up in my office at about 2:30 in the morning and just started writing. What came of it was a letter. It wasn't to anybody in particular, but it was also to everyone at the same time.

The letter was to my coaches and teammates, my family and friends, Raider Nation and the city of Las Vegas. I just wanted to let everyone know how much they meant to me and how grateful I was to be a part of this team. There was no intention of sharing it with anyone, it helped me fall back asleep and maintain my standard of rehab.

The next day, Will Compton and I got to talking and I ended up sharing that letter with him. He said it needed to be public and gave me the courage to take a step out of my comfort zone and connect with our community.

One of the biggest pieces of advice I'll never forget him saying was "You aren't as important as you think you are. Most people will blow right past this story and never think twice about it. You owe it to the people who can feel inspired and connect with this on their own journey. Don't overthink it; those six inches between your ears are your biggest enemy, not some keyboard warrior." No one cares. Go all in.

It's okay to sometimes adopt a "me against the world" mentality. Developing talent or overcoming a setback is a lonely road at times. It's not a road that everyone can travel on either. Many people give up. Usually because they haven't clearly defined their priorities or goals. They haven't created standards that propel them forward. I'm not only talking about mental toughness, I'm talking about physical toughness as well.

As an athlete, if you're a dozen games into the season, everyone on your team is in pain. That's just the nature of football. Fans know this. But fans also only care what happens on Sundays. They don't care about getting treatments for nagging muscle pulls, massive bruises, sprains, or strains for bodies that have been repeatedly punished for weeks upon weeks. They just want you to win, and most of them don't care about what it takes Monday through Saturday to make that happen.

The ironic thing is that as a player, this is understood. It needs no explanation. You owe it to the fans to do the hard work when nobody is watching and on those days when nobody cares. You also owe it to your family, coaches, teammates, and most important of all, to yourself.

Two Cups of Talent

Here's a great way to think about the difference between talent and effort.

Suppose you have two same-sized cups with water inside. Cup A and Cup B compete against each other. The overall size of the cups represents potential, and the amount of water inside represents their ability to execute on the same challenge they both face. The two starting points of water in the cup represent the cup's talent level. Cup A starts three-quarters filled with more talent than Cup B, which is only half filled. Cup A succeeds at every task through talent alone. That cup stays three-quarters filled. Cup A, because it enjoys early success, never feels the need to fill itself even higher.

Cup B is constantly stressed, always trying to find ways to get a few more drops of water to successfully accomplish challenges. Cup B gets into a routine of figuring out how to accomplish one task at a time by creativity, discipline, and maximizing every drop of talent. It gets into the habit of finding a few more drops of water after each challenge it faces. Over time, Cup B slowly fills a drop or two at a time.

This can go on for years, Cup A effortlessly skating by, and Cup B having to align its heart, mind, and body to continue. But what happens when Cup B reaches three-quarters filled? What happens when their talents are equal? What happens when there's a test that requires more water than either cup holds? What happens when the stress of the test outweighs the amount of talent in the cup?

Here's what happens. The two cups are going to rely on what they've done in the past to continue forward. Cup A is going to struggle, get frustrated, and most likely quit because this is something out of routine. Cup A is going to stay at three-quarters filled and fail at that critical moment. Cup B is also going to keep doing what it knows, to grind. Cup B is going to see the challenge and smile because there is a way to pass the test. That relentless pursuit, Cup B's Grindset, has become a habit that will create ongoing growth a couple drops at a time.

The moral is that you should embrace the challenge. Embrace the difficulties of the journey to getting better. Embrace the Grindset.

There's no point in comparing yourself to someone more talented or more successful than you, just lock in on running your own race and getting better 1% at a time. You can't cheat the grind, and once you align your mindset and heartset, your growth is inevitable.

• • •

Ask yourself these questions if you want to overcome the Grindset Crucible.

- Do you have what it takes within you to commit to your personal version of the Grindset? What elements do you already have that serve you well to incorporate the Grindset into your life's goals?
- Your Grindset is already inside of you. How will you summon it? How deep are you willing to dig to bring it out? Are you willing to fully commit to yourself?
- What kind of adversity must you overcome to climb that metaphorical mountain? Are you easily distracted? Do you talk a good game but then don't take the real action required to succeed? Do you hang out with people who can't advance your Grindset goals? Are you taking supreme ownership of your mindset and heartset?

Next, don't worry about if you're talented enough or not to succeed, but truly ask yourself if your character is where it needs to be in order to achieve your goals.

You must develop talent and character in tandem with each other. You can become physically gifted if you work hard at it in an intentional manner. But how often do you work on your character? It goes beyond asking "Am I a good person?" and goes straight to personal accountability.

Until you work on your physical, spiritual, and emotional well-being, Grindset challenges will be much harder to overcome. You must apply the right amount of effort and attention to each for your given circumstances and goals. Finding ways to fill your cup the right way will give you the tools you need to conquer your Grindset Crucible.

The Support
Crucible

This is my command: Love each other.

John 15:17

When times are tough, do you know who's in your corner? Which people can you rely on to pick you up when you can't do it yourself?

They are the ones who know you inside and out and have committed to you just as much as you have committed to them. And that means a commitment on the highest level, which only a few people in your life will ever reach.

It's easy to be a friend and supportive when things are going well. But true friendship and support can only be forged under extreme heat and pressure.

The Support Crucible is all about forging your inner circle. You must have friends and family in place who are going to support you regardless of your successes or failures. Quality over quantity is critical. Fortunately, over time, you develop a knack for knowing who really cares and who's just along for the ride.

Think of the levels of support you receive as a series of circles, one large circle leading to a smaller circle, which leads to another smaller circle and so on. At the outermost circle are the people who are very casual in their relationship with you. This may be people who only follow you on social media, your coworkers, or people you may run into rarely from time to time. These are your *casual acquaintances.*

The next innermost circle are friends you see, perhaps on a regular basis, as time allows. You share lots of friends and beliefs in common. This may be college frat or sorority friends, people you grew up with in your neighborhood whom you still see when you come home to visit, coaches you really connected with, or people you see at church every week. I call these your *seasonal friends*.

The next circle consists of your immediate family members and closest friends. You see and talk to them often, sometimes almost daily. You invest in real conversations with them about things that are important to both of you, and you're bound by shared memories but not necessarily by blood. You're honest with each other and both of you take time to actively LISTEN to each other. These are your *lifelong friends*.

The next circle is *you*. You must be willing to put yourself at the center of your support universe. This is not selfish in any way. Just the opposite. If you're not fully actualized within yourself, you have no shot of supporting other people in your life.

Here's the thing, the circles don't stop there. One more circle inward is the Holy Spirit, or *Jesus Christ*. My faith as a Christian is a pure and driving force that influences all that I do. The support of my Savior means everything to me and allows me to be the best possible version of myself. More than anything else, I draw upon His support to help me overcome adversity. The power of the Holy Spirit fuels God's will and gives me strength to believe I can accomplish anything.

I hope this visual helps you understand that when adversity cuts deep, it will cut through a lot of those outer circles. Those acquaintances and seasonal friends most likely won't be there for you during the crucibles you encounter. Sometimes, that lifelong friend and family circle or your own circle can handle the challenge, but when all else fails and you're stripped of everything protecting you, that's when real change happens. That's when you really find out what YOU'RE made of, and who's really in your corner when times seem the darkest.

It's a Lonely Road, Man . . .

Playing professional football is absolutely a dream job. I wouldn't trade it for the world. But it comes at a cost. Aside from the physical challenges, there are a lot of mental and emotional challenges as well.

It's not talked about much in the NFL, but the stress and strain you go through is considerable. In a best case, you learn to grow into that part of the game. I envy players and coaches who have mastered the mental part. In many ways, it's what separates good players from great players.

There are lots of components to the mental part of the game that challenge players. Some must work hard at the responsibility that comes with a lack of privacy from always being in the public eye. Others are distracted by fame, money, and blind adulation.

For me, the biggest thing I still wrestle with is that it's a lonely road, man.

It's a lonely road.

That may strike you as odd, and in some ways it is. While football is very much a team game, and I'm extremely close to all my brothers on the field, we play on teams of high-performing individuals, each on our own unique journey. Trades, injuries, retirements, and other life events are why the NFL stands for "Not For Long" in the locker rooms. On the surface, we're very close, but deep down, I think there's also a sense of being alone more times than we may admit.

There are also other forms of loneliness that compound those feelings as well.

When you play pro football, you're very much in a bubble. On game day, you're an alpha dog in the public eye. But when the lights go off, it's just you. Fans at the game go home to their families. Everyone watching on TV changes the channel, gathers around the dinner table, walks their dog, hangs out with their friends and neighbors, or kicks back and preps for the week ahead.

People have a hard time relating to the sacrifice that comes in the form of loneliness when you play this game. If you have money, followers, or success it's automatically assumed those things create happiness and fulfillment.

That's not the case. The two aren't necessarily linked. Like anything else, finding happiness and fulfillment requires work on your part *and* investing in others.

The people in your inner circle need to break through the professional football player stigmas and stereotypes to have real and vulnerable conversations with you. As a player, you need to reciprocate by letting them in.

These people are in your corner to pick you up when you're down as well as be brutally honest and ground you when you're on cloud nine.

NFL athletes live in a world with the highest of highs and the lowest of lows. The great irony is that the path to greatness requires a level of consistency and a middle ground. This creates a constant mental, physical, and emotional battle to find that space and stay there.

It's essential to have a circle of discipleship and support where you're held accountable to consistently being yourself. Having high character conversations with the people you love isn't always easy. But if you don't make a serious effort to regularly communicate like this, the roller coaster of emotions you constantly live with as part of the NFL will chew you up and spit you out.

What complicates things is that as an NFL player, there's an intensity of time, focus, and energy that makes it more challenging to develop close relationships, find people who genuinely support you, and in turn, people you can genuinely support. You accept this when you play the game. Your life is not a normal life. It's not written into any contract but isolation is part of what comes from being in the NFL bubble.

Undrafted Day

I can't think of a better story that paints a picture for you regarding the kind of people you want around you than what happened to me on Draft Day in the spring of 2019. It didn't exactly go the way I wanted it to, but I learned a valuable lesson from it all.

Draft Day is a graduation day. You go from college football to the league! When you're drafted, it's a golden ticket and moment of validation from your years of work and sacrifice that gives you the opportunity to possibly play in the NFL.

In anticipation of getting drafted, my friends and family gathered for a draft party at my parent's home. There was a buzz that day, everyone was kind of on edge, especially me. This was a confirmation that everything I'd worked for to this point would be recognized and valued. At least one team, and maybe more, would see that I was a perfect fit for their system, and that my talent, effort, and attitude would put me over the top and into the NFL.

And then, the unthinkable happened.

For four hours we were glued to the TV, watching everyone celebrate their moment.

But I never got the call. I didn't get drafted.

What could have been the best weekend of my life turned into the worst experience of my life. It was an awkward, crushing feeling I had never felt before. I was shell-shocked. My fiancé Alexa was there, and she knew what it meant. My high school coach Westy was there, and he knew what it meant, as did some of my closest lifelong friends.

After some quick meetings and phone calls in the privacy of my parents' bedroom, I went out to the living room where everyone was waiting to share the news. I was offered an undrafted free agent contract with the Silver and Black, and I was heading out to Alameda, California, to try and become a Oakland Raider. I think I was smiling and upbeat on the outside as I told everyone, but on the inside, I was gut shot. It's not the path I was expecting, but I'll be forever grateful to the Raiders for cracking open the door for me. That's all I needed.

The off-season program was scheduled to start 10 short days after the draft was over. But before I could even think about attending, I needed to get my head right.

Although everyone at the draft party cheered the news, in my mind, I fully believed that being an undrafted free agent rookie fullback was only going to net me a $10,000 signing bonus, a cup of coffee at the Raiders training facility, and a quick trip back home after they cut me.

That's when my support system saved me, and therein lies the lesson of the Support Crucible.

My dad and I sat down on the front porch of our home the morning after the draft. I could fool lots of other people, but I couldn't fool him. He knew exactly how I felt. He knew how much I'd sacrificed over the years, the dreams I had of playing pro football, and just as important how part of me felt I'd let everyone down when I wasn't drafted.

My dad didn't coddle me. He didn't pat me on the back, ask me how I was doing, or if I was okay. Instead of wallowing in disappointment, which was useless at that point, my dad asked me,

---

"Are you ready to go and take on a grown man's job?"

We talked about a lot of other things, but that one question snapped me back to reality. My dad, my biggest supporter, locked me back into my goal and yanked me out of the hole I had crawled into.

It was like hooking up jumper cables to my motivation and the perfect reminder that despite the freaking marathon of commitment I'd already gone through my entire life up to this point, it wasn't enough to earn the external validation I was looking for.

Most of all, it reminded me that no matter what the outcome of the camp, I was still loved by lots of people. Their relentless support lit a fire in me. I dug deep to channel my God-given talent and to say thank you for that belief.

From that talk with my dad, my head and my purpose immediately came into focus. I was ready to strap up my helmet, step onto the field, and take a job I had not been given.

Thanks to everyone's support, I went to that camp with my head screwed on straight, worked my ass off, and signed with the Raiders as an undrafted free agent on May 3, 2019.

Support Is a Two-Way Street

The NFL is an unusual type of support system. On the one hand, as a player you're part of a brotherhood of men. On the other, if you're not strong or talented enough, you'll be left behind as they decisively find somebody else to do your job.

No hard feelings. That's just the way the NFL is. That's what you sign up for.

While supporting your team and your teammates is crucial, you need to give serious thought to how much you invest your support in others as well.

Understand this. Support is a two-way street. You can't get and not give.

Unless you do, in the end, you'll lose and wind up without any support at all.

When I tore my ACL, Alexa flew out to Las Vegas to take care of me. My dad took time off work and came out as well, while my mom, Chris, held down the fort at home. My dad, more than anyone else, knew I was at my most vulnerable as a pro athlete who had been reduced to barely being able to walk. My lifelong friends sent me countless texts and called me day after day to check on me.

Their love and support fueled my recovery. It was because of them that I gained intensity and fueled my courage and confidence so that I could make a full recovery and play pro football again.

I also knew that even if I fell short of that goal, they would still be there for me. The quality of their character fueled the quality of my character and continues to do so to this day.

It's a matter of priorities, and I've always tried to be there for them. It's a challenge because distance and time are often stressed, but it matters to us. We travel the distance, and we make time. I view it as an investment that has paid dividends many times over.

That support didn't just come out of nowhere. It's been built over many years. I've made it a point to be there for those important people in my life any way I can.

Mutual support is a part of my DNA, and something that has carried over to my teammates at all levels. Being there, listening, and communicating is as much of a skill as lifting weights, learning plays, and practicing hard every day.

Even after my injury, I made it a point to stay close with my teammates to support them with a late season push that ultimately led to a playoff berth. I couldn't be on the field, but I could act as a sounding board, help them fight through physical, mental, emotional, and spiritual challenges they faced, knowing that their victories were also a victory for me. Just like my dad had done for me, when needed I also held them accountable to a higher standard as well.

The point is this.

You shouldn't have to go through your trials all alone. In fact, it's not healthy. When anxiety, depression, spiritual doubts, or setbacks happen, your burdens are considerably lessened whether you're on the giving or the receiving end of that support.

We all go through peaks and valleys. Everyone has great days and bad. The point is to share these moments with others, to be there for one another and truly experience the journey y'all walk together.

When it's time to split paths, wish each other well, but while you're walking side by side, give without the intent to receive. Hold nothing back to your support system; BE YOU!

That genuine relationship will mature the both of you for the better, and prepare you for that inevitable next crucible, whatever it may be.

• • •

- Do you have clearly defined relationship circles in your life? Chances are they are developed to a certain degree, but are you clear about who the people are you can trust without hesitation, and those who play a lesser role in your life?

- Think about the last time you encountered extreme adversity in your life. Who was there for you? Who rallied to you without asking? I've been fortunate because I've learned a lot about my inner circle through the adversity I've faced by not getting drafted, and which people responded when I went down with my ACL injury.

Also think about how you've supported others in the past. Have you done everything you could, given the circumstances at the time, to be as supportive as possible? Be honest with yourself. Deep down, only you know the nature of your heart.

One final thing to think about . . .

Even if I didn't have these people in my life, and I am beyond grateful that I do, I know that I'll never walk through adversity alone because of my relationship with Jesus Christ. I can't even begin to tell you the level of peace and comfort that brings me.

The Leadership
Crucible

Very truly I tell you, no servant is greater than his master,
nor is a messenger greater than the one who sent him.

John 13:16

Here's the question I'm faced with now.

How do I remain an effective and engaged team leader when I'm recovering from a torn ACL?

Talk about a challenge. Talk about adversity. It has led me to the most difficult leadership challenge in my life. My entire life I've led by example. I've paid my dues through hard work and gaining respect before speaking up. Now, how can I lead from the bench? How can I help a team win without contributing in an active role?

A quarterback is a natural leader on any team, sports or otherwise. The wolf out in front of the pack. The quarterback calls the plays, decides when action is warranted, and directly impacts the outcome of each play.

It's slightly different when you're a fullback. On any given play, you're expected to hit people hard, do your specific job, and do it over again (often without a pat on the back). You're less visible but still vital to the outcome. So, if you're a guy like me, you look to lead in other ways, from the middle of the pack.

The Leadership Decision

Not everyone wants to lead. Some are happy being a role player on the team. Others quietly do their job and take direction well. When they execute well, the team does well. Truth be told, if everyone decided they wanted to lead, nothing would get accomplished. You must have a chain of command, whether it's a football team, a business, or even in your own family.

Some people are natural-born leaders. They seek and thrive as leaders. They are not afraid to accept responsibility, speak their mind, and carry the challenge of leading others.

If you decide to be a leader, there are several ways to accomplish this. As I mentioned, it's one thing to be a quarterback and lead your team, but much different for a player like me. I'm a role player, some weeks it's a big role and some weeks it's small, but it's a role nonetheless.

Because of my role, I look for less overt ways to lead. That means I'm the guy in practice who makes sure to talk with everyone, ensuring they're focused because good practices often lead to great games. There's a balance between building personal relationships, trust, and accountability with the guys. They know that I truly care about them, and if they trust I'm doing my job at 100%, they can do theirs with nothing held back.

I'm also the guy in the weight room quietly going hard, setting an example and a standard for others to follow.

If you want to be a leader, you have to be prepared to set an example through your devotion to hard work. It's impossible to lead others to their best lives if you're not willing to put in the work to get to your best life. The example you set gets noticed. It means everything.

I've found that it's possible to be a leader no matter what position you hold on your team. You can lead from the front as a quarterback does. You can lead from the middle, much like I do. Or you can lead from the rear, finding ways to contribute, even when you make little or no contribution on the field.

As I recover from my injury, I've had to look at how I can keep contributing to being a leader on my team. It's not easy, but if I'm willing to contribute, and I am, attitude is everything.

I've discovered that you must be willing to take some risks. I think that's what great leaders do. They analyze options, listen to trusted input from others, and then make decisions. It can be scary as you grow into this role. Getting outside the six inches between your ears can be intimidating at first, especially when you're the new guy and talking to a bunch of high-performing, alpha male teammates.

Being a leader evolves over time. Respect the totem pole. Put in your hours and apply the gifts you've been given, physical and otherwise. Demonstrate that not only are you balling for yourself, but more importantly, you're playing for all your teammates as well.

Having others respect and embrace your leadership is earned over time.

I've received a lot of awards and accolades as a player. But I can honestly say the one that has meant more to me than any other was being named the Raiders team captain for the 2021 season. I went from an undrafted free agent to team captain in three years, and that honor, as voted on by my teammates, validated everything I believe in as a leader. Wearing that *C* on my chest was a representation of the trust and hard work I had put in to try and become the best leader I could as a part of our team.

Much of my leadership style was built on two pillars: communication and inspiring belief.

Great Leaders Are Great Communicators

It's impossible to be a great leader unless you're a great communicator.

You can do this even with a toasted ACL. Like any other challenge in life, you need to learn how to adjust and adapt to the circumstances you've been blessed with and challenged to overcome.

When I went down with my injury, everything I was doing on the field, like catching passes, running the ball, blocking, and maintaining energy and intensity for all of our players, was gone.

After I accepted the physical loss, I needed to accept that I'd need to adjust mentally so I could keep contributing as a member of the team. With my physical abilities on hold for the time being, I needed to become a more effective communicator to compensate.

Leadership does not operate in a messaging vacuum. How you communicate with your team members relies heavily on tone, frequency, and specificity. In some ways, my torn ACL allowed me to slow down, think deeper about how to connect with my teammates, and lead by example in other ways. I started by becoming a better listener.

I went to practices and began coaching our guys by spending more time in the film room and asking leading questions to get the most out of our film cut-ups. I remained genuine in showing every player on that team that I cared about him. Instead of attending team meetings as I could based on my recovery regimen, I adjusted my recovery schedule around team meetings and the rest of the team's schedule.

In that way, I communicated with those guys, without saying a word, that they were my priority. My actions placed them above my own needs, which I think great leaders should do.

This also helped my rehab because I could stay close to them. Just like I served them, they also were there serving me. ACL injuries are a dime a dozen nowadays, so even though this is my first major injury, the guys around me were constantly giving advice through personal experience. The investment in each other was mutual, and in season, this was a critical part of getting over the mental hump of dealing with a significant injury.

The hardest part was watching the remaining games from my couch. I couldn't attend games in person because my knee would swell up if I was on it for any length of time. I also couldn't fly for away games due to swelling at altitude.

I missed—and I mean really missed—being in the middle of the pre-game huddle, spilling my guts, and giving everything I had (however cheesy it came out) to my motivational speech that fired us up before we took the field. Cutting my guys loose and hoping for the best on those Sundays was the hardest part of my recovery.

Regardless of the outcome, I also knew as a leader that I would be there at the start of the new week, doing my part to help my team win. I could still help with our preparation, just not the performance.

Finding a new way to connect and communicate strengthened and validated my thoughts on leadership.

Being a great communicator as part of being a leader can be unforgiving at times. You work hard to find the right words and understand that what you say often directly impacts how your team responds.

But when you find the right words and then see them translate on the field, it means everything.

Great Leaders Inspire Belief

The ability to lead others relies on the talent of inspiring others in their mission and in themselves.

There are several parts of inspiring belief, but it starts with you. You can't lead others if you can't do a great job of leading and inspiring belief in yourself. Asking others to do it when you can't do it for yourself is not genuine. You need to be all in with yourself and your goals without ever asking someone else to join you.

I inspire belief through my faith and humility to ask for help, energy, purpose, and divine power. This supercharges my efforts. I urge you to think about what creates passion in you, whether it is your God or some other force so that you can discover the highest levels of inspiration as well.

I have also found strength through the adversity I've faced. For example, I've wrestled with being adopted my entire life. I fought with the notion of being rejected by my biological parents. That created low self-esteem and anxiety that I have continued to face, although much less now that I realize the circumstances and have a much different perspective on that part of my life.

I've replaced many of those bad feelings with gratitude based on the family I have now, my standing in the community, and my accomplishments on and off the field. It's a unique way that I've inspired belief in myself.

Aside from the mental part of inspiring belief in myself, there are several other things I do as a matter of routine. They'll work well for you, too.

Here's how to inspire belief in yourself . . .

- **Work hard to attain supreme physical condition.** As a pro athlete, this is a given, but you need to be aware of it anyway. No matter what you do in life, when you take care of your physical being, you'll feel better emotionally and spiritually.
- **Develop an unstoppable and contagious work ethic.** This applies to all parts of your life. Don't waste time or focus on busywork. Instead, focus on work that will produce the greatest return for you. In my case, I'm able to make conscious decisions about my routine so the consistent work, attitude, and purpose speaks for itself. I relate it to water always finding its way downhill. Somehow, some way it always flows to where it should be.
- **Create a positive manifesting mindset.** Pray. Meditate. Flood your being with messages you need to build confidence. That will translate into actions to produce the game-winning outcomes you want. Positive self-talk is necessary in reinforcing your belief. We all have self-doubt, but when you create positive messages to repeat and fall back on when times get tough, you create a strong shield of self-accountability.
- **Dominate your preparation phase.** Practice, practice, and practice more. That is the key! But that's not enough. You must practice the right way. Do not just go through the motions. Bring focus, intensity, and

purpose in the same order of magnitude that you bring to your real-life challenges. For me, when I practice the way that I play, the game becomes easier, and I become a more dominant force. It's one of the keys to my long-term success. I only know one way to practice, and I only know one way to play.

- **Extend inspiring belief into all areas of your life.** Stay on point. Live your brand. Don't box up your passion into one part of your life. Let that inspiration overflow into relationships and actions throughout your life. For me, that led to speaking about financial literacy, professional development, and mental health to underserved youth and kids going through adoption.

How to inspire belief in others . . .

- **Help your staff, teammates, and coaches believe in the best versions of themselves.** Best versions are required to win, and if you do it the right way, this mindset is contagious. Set an expectation that when someone meets you, this is what they will hear. You and your message become inseparable, and those who seek you out will be receptive to the "best version" reinforcement you give them.
- **Help others find and feel a daily, consistent, and never-ending purpose.** If you have an ongoing relationship with these people, give thought to how you can integrate their purpose with yours. There is a multiplier effect when you add the combined purpose of two, three, four, or more people all locked in to the same mission.

- **What is the collective vision?** For any team I play on, it is winning a Super Bowl. Make sure everyone you work with knows exactly what the vision is. When everyone you work with or have a relationship with combines the day-to-day purpose with a long-term ultimate purpose, you produce harmony and consistent results over several levels and timeframes.

How to inspire belief in all instances . . .

- **Create an unlimited scope of inspiration.** Exhaust as many avenues as possible. Dare to imagine and dream of the things you want and use that as jet fuel to propel your life forward.
- **Look for opportunities to share God's love.** Draw strength and purpose from your faith. Use your faith to inspire belief in everyone you meet.
- **Be consistent and clear.** Always stay on point. Keep your messages simple so nothing is lost in translation. The impetus is on you as the originator to get your point across to anyone willing to listen.
- **Understand the connected nature of your world.** Every person is connected in many ways. When you speak and act, be aware that your messages will echo, creating vibrations that will unlock doors and lead to places you never could imagine.
- **Maintain a consistent and honorable set of values.** There should be no doubt about what you will and won't tolerate. Remain consistent in your efforts and what you stand for. Choose important base values such as kindness, compassion, loyalty, honesty, honor,

counsel, and fortitude. Then build on those to create the best version of yourself

How you inspire belief must be tailored to who you are and whom you want to inspire. In my life, there are three primary groups of people whom I want to impact this way. Each requires a different approach.

As an athlete. I think about my relationship with others based on whether they see me as a team captain, a fullback, a teammate, my team's fan, an NFL fan, or any other capacity.

As a member of my family. I am a husband, a son, a brother, and eventually, a father.

As an educator. I consider my role as a speaker, the founder of my nonprofit, and in coaching my youth in the game of life.

While I am the same person in all instances, I take into consideration how I impact each of the roles I have in my life, and then I communicate and inspire belief in the ways I think will be most effective in a given situation.

• • •

One of the many challenges of becoming an effective leader is that you must also develop several character traits. Here are several of the traits I think that are important to study and master.

- Focus less on talent and more on your standards.
- Make sure your priorities have a high degree of purpose.
- Be a dreamer.
- Be a grinder. Be stubborn. Refuse to give in.

- Practice mindful sustained motivation.
- Put in real work to produce real results.
- Make a daily deposit.
- Be Godly and righteous.
- Dare to think and be different.
- Channel others' doubts into your positive energy.
- Remember the definition of *insanity*.
- Remain overly focused.
- Turn interest into motivation and motivation into purpose.
- Finish your fights and fight to the finish.
- Win lots of small one-on-one battles.
- Figure out what you need to be perfectly placed to dominate.
- Become addicted to the journey, not the destination.
- Do whatever it takes to align your mind, body, and spirit
- Do your hard work in the lab and behind the scenes.
- Understand what it means to be patiently impatient.

Think about what character traits you value. How many do you already incorporate into your life? Are there traits that no longer serve you well or that you can swap out for something more effective for who you are now?

Great leaders are able to overcome adversity by thinking in advance about the things I've laid out in this crucible.

Spend time getting to know yourself in a leadership role. Great leaders don't happen by accident. Like anything else in life, they work at it, and so should you.

The Discipline
Crucible

No discipline seems pleasant at the time, but painful.
Later on, however, it produces a harvest of righteousness
and peace for those who have been trained by it.

Hebrews 12:11

The most difficult battles you'll face are the ones inside your head. All pro football players have amazing physical gifts, but it's the ones who understand the discipline of routine and setting a standard that have the best careers.

Discipline means you don't compromise. It's about sustained emotional intensity, with a decent amount of stubbornness mixed in, creating a focused mindset to give you the best chance of transforming dreams to reality.

Always Keep the Main Thing, the Main Thing

Professional football is filled with distractions. No big revelation there. That's life, everyone deals with it when you're chasing greatness.

It's how you react to these distractions that determines your success. Just because you're the most talented does not automatically translate to being the most successful. Pro sports of all kinds are filled with stories about guys who let the shiny objects of the big leagues blind them from what got them there in the first place.

That's why the best advice I can give you about discipline is always to keep the main thing, the main thing.

In my case, that applies to football, but more importantly, life.

You owe that to yourself, your team, your coaches, and all the people who have supported you since you were little.

It would be incredibly selfish of me or any other pro athlete to squander their talents on distractions instead of focusing on the main thing. And in my case, the main thing is to play football to the best of my ability, every day, until I retire.

Discipline may show the fruits of its labor on Sundays in the fall, but that's not where it's developed. Discipline must be your constant companion every time you practice, during the workouts after practice, and in the evenings when you're studying game tape.

Coaches can try to instill discipline, but discipline comes from within. The only one who can enforce discipline on you is you. Coaches can create standards, and you can work to those standards, but discipline is different.

Talent gets you to the game. But it's discipline that wins the game. You will see the results when you're disciplined and passionate enough to put the work in. However, if you think you can shortcut the process, you will lose regularly.

Discipline is the main thing.

And as I've already said, you must always keep the main thing, the main thing.

The 17-Inch Standard

After I tore my ACL, our team went into a tailspin, losing five of the next six games. It's a tough thing to endure, especially when you have a fan show up at the Raiders' practice facility with a bag over his head, because at the time, you're only one game below .500!

We all needed a reminder of what it took for us to get off to such a great start to our season. Some sort of reset button to hit and get our swagger back. Our Hall of Fame defensive line coach Rod Marinelli gave us precisely what we were looking for.

Coach Marinelli handed me a packet of motivational materials that included a famous story about legendary Cal Poly Pomona baseball coach John Scolinos.

As the story goes, Coach Scolinos was scheduled as a keynote speaker at a national baseball convention. In the audience were coaches from all levels, including other high schools, colleges, the minor leagues, and Major League Baseball.

Coach Scolinos stepped to the podium wearing a life-sized home plate around his neck. At first, he didn't even acknowledge his unusual prop, but eventually, he let everyone in on its significance.

The point he made was this.

When you're a coach, the size of home plate does not change. It will always be 17 inches wide whether you play in Little League, high school, or in the majors. The size of home plate will not change, and it won't apologize if you can throw a strike or not.

So, as a coach, it's up to you to teach plate discipline and the game in a way that does not deviate from the 17-inch standard. Any time you let your team or your players slack off, or deviate from the set standard, you've lowered the bar. It doesn't matter if it's the star player or last one on the bench, you coach everyone to the standard you set to maintain the integrity of your program. That requires discipline in how you and your players approach the game.

It was the perfect example of how discipline must apply to your life no matter what "game" you're playing, and exactly what we needed to reset as a team.

The Relationship Between Discipline and Standards

Although discipline and standards are linked at the hip, they are different, and it's essential to understand how they work together.

Standards are the controllable performance levels you hold yourself accountable to in whatever goal you're pursuing. You create more than an expectation. You create an unbreakable bond from which you do not waver.

For example, as a football player, you set a goal of wanting to get stronger, and to do that, you know you must hit the weights hard five days a week to get to the next level. That's something you can control and commit to. You can measure your improvement by keeping track of how much extra weight you lift or how many additional reps you do from one month to the next.

Discipline is the X-factor that allows you to meet your standard on the toughest days. Discipline is more about the consistency of how you show up regardless of circumstances. If you don't have the required discipline to rise to the standard you or your team agreed upon, you're setting yourself up for failure.

An even better example is recovering from my ACL injury. If I want to get back to 100% as quickly as possible, I've got to follow a strict regimen of exercises and workouts to shorten the number of days I end up in the training room.

Rehabbing is a lonely process, and there are so many days when you don't want to do the work. You're down because your body is a big part of your livelihood, and it won't respond the way it does when you're healthy. Those are the days when discipline means everything to your rehab.

Setting the proper standards means little if you don't have the discipline to execute them. They must work together to get you where you want to go.

By its very nature, discipline is a form of adversity because you must be mentally strong to fight through your low energy, low motivation days. And it's winning the battle of discipline that gets you through those times.

Applying a high standard and discipline can also transform you into a role model for your teammates, family members, and coworkers. The right attitude can inspire others to act the same way.

When you apply standards and discipline the right way, you become a de facto leader, even from the sidelines, as others look to you as someone they can count on when times are the toughest.

1% Days

Every football player and many people in life would do well to look to Jerry Rice as the GOAT when it comes to discipline in your work.

Jerry Rice was gifted with natural abilities, but when he decided to set a Hall of Fame standard for himself and develop the discipline to see it through, he became the best wide receiver the game has ever seen. He was also one of the most quotable and inspirational players ever.

He's famous for saying:

> *"Today I will do what others won't, so tomorrow I will do what others can't."*

Here's another:

> *"I was always willing to work; I was not the fastest or biggest player, but I was determined to be the best football player I could be on the football field, and I think I was able to accomplish that through hard work."*

If those don't sound like using discipline to its highest advantage, I don't know what does.

Jerry compounded his disciplined effort over an extended timeframe, consistently getting just a little bit better every day. My strength coach in college called this "Marginal Gains."

I like to think of that consistent growth over time as 1% Days. Those small incremental advancements don't seem like much growth on their own. But when you add 1% + 1% + 1% and so on for days and months at a time, the changes are monumental. It's just like compounding interest in an investment account, which many successful investors claim is the eighth wonder of the world.

Jerry Rice didn't make it into the Hall of Fame on talent alone. He accomplished that incredible goal by understanding that discipline + standards + time + 1% every day = The Hall of Fame.

I believe in the concept of 1% Days, which is why I always bring the same level of passion, energy, and charisma to the field every time I practice and play. Everyone can do it when they're feeling good; the best ones do it when the odds are stacked against them.

To me, that's the key to overcoming the challenges associated with discipline. You turn bad days into good ones by setting high standards and then implement elements of discipline to create your best outcomes.

The Broken Rib Conundrum

From my firsthand account, I can tell you it really hurts when you've got broken ribs and you sneeze.

During my second year in the league, I was crushing it, living out my dreams. I was building on the momentum I created my rookie season, going from being an undrafted rookie to a Pro Bowl alternate. This year was *my* year. I was firing on all cylinders and was right at the top of Pro Football Focus week in and week out for my position.

Midway through the season, we had a game against the Los Angeles Chargers on the road at the team's new palace, SoFi Stadium. The game was odd from the start because this was at the height of Covid-19, and there were no fans in the stands. We wanted to exploit a mismatch against them, and I was a big part of that plan. It was Alec Ingold and Josh Jacobs versus the Chargers' linebackers and safeties, and we had every intention of running the ball down their throats.

We were near their goal line, huddled up, and called our G-Lead play that is a "pin and pull" run using our tight end Jason Witten to block the Chargers' defensive end. With Jason blocking down, and our guard pulling to kick out the corner, my job was to lead Josh Jacobs through the hole and block the outside linebacker. The thing about this type of play is the guy I'm blocking is trained to keep his outside shoulder pads free, so the running back doesn't get outside of him. I told you I was firing on all cylinders, hitting people, and running through blocks like an animal. On that play, I hit the defender so hard on his outside shoulder that we both crashed to the ground.

Josh Jacobs went outside of us and into the endzone untouched. But I didn't escape unscathed. While a defensive lineman was pursuing the play, the 300-pounder jumped over a pile of players and his knee landed on my ribs.

Not gonna lie: that kinda hurt.

Oh Lord, did that hurt!

Guys celebrated after the touchdown until they saw me lying on the ground. Derek Carr, Rodney Hudson, and Witten all gathered around me to see if I was okay. Turns out, that answer was "no!"

I cracked my eighth and tenth ribs, and all I could do when it happened was lay flat on my back and look straight up at the ceiling of the big, shiny, brand new six-billion dollar SoFi Stadium with a couple of broken ribs to remember that moment.

I went to the hospital for x-rays to ensure I didn't have a punctured lung and then made it back in time to join my teammates for the flight back home. Everyone was patting me on the back and telling me how they would miss me for the next four or five weeks, hoping that I could return in time for our big time playoff run.

Except, that being out of action for four or five weeks wasn't part of my plan.

On that flight home, I made up my mind I would do whatever it took to help my team reach the playoffs.

I walked into the training room the next day, much to everyone's surprise. It hurt to move, walk, and roll over. Heck, it hurt to breathe!

From the training room tables I saw a handful of guys heading out to the indoor practice field. I had asked what was going on over there, and one of the trainers told me that the team was auditioning a half dozen replacement fullbacks to play while I was out.

C'mon dog!

I had worked too hard to prove to people I was good enough to play, and now I was being treated like an interchangeable piece of the puzzle?

I don't think so!

I looked at the trainers and told them I was going to play, broken ribs and all. They warned me about reinjuring the ribs and possibly puncturing my lung, but I didn't care. I told them I had played 30 games or so in the NFL to that point and this was the first time I had broken ribs. Then I defiantly asked what the chances of that happening again were. But I didn't wait for an answer I might not want to hear. The training staff grabbed me a bulletproof Kevlar® vest to wrap around my ribs so that I could practice and get ready to play the following week against our division rivals the Denver Broncos.

I put the vest on and walked out on the field to start practicing. It hurt to walk. It hurt to jog. It hurt during every part of practice that week.

Here's the point.

I had set a high standard for myself. And I had created an equally high level of discipline. I mentally conditioned myself in the moments after I broke my ribs to put the pain aside because I was going to play. Period, end of discussion.

I sent a message to my teammates to let them know how much football mattered to me by toughing it out. If I could play through broken ribs and that level of adversity, as a leader, I wanted them to match my efforts with their own high level of grit and determination.

How bad did I want it?

The day before the Broncos game, I struggled through the entire practice during our team walkthrough. But by far, the worst part of that whole experience was when I sneezed. That brought me to my knees in tears because the pain was so bad. It was a jolt of reality the day before the game, knowing even the slightest movement was going to be magnified for the foreseeable future.

I didn't miss a snap during that entire game the next day. Not gonna lie: I didn't have one of those Michael Jordan flu game performances. I played like garbage and didn't impact the game against the Broncos, or the following week against the Chiefs. But I was proud of the discipline it took to fight through my broken ribs. It took everything I had to fight through that adversity.

I proved something to myself and didn't let excuses get in my way of the standards and level of discipline I had set for myself. It turned out to be a different kind of victory for me, but was just as important as several other athletic accomplishments in my life.

Spirit, Body, Mind, Emotion

I want to leave you with one last thought about discipline.

Discipline is the result of reflecting on and finding peace in four critical elements of your life.

- **Spirit.** Your first priority is to nourish your spirit through prayer early in the morning, late at night, or at whatever time of day works best for you according to your beliefs. Our deepest spiritual values define our purposes, and the best way to bring substance to your life is to pray and reflect on the answers you need to help you overcome adversity and maintain discipline.

- **Body.** Your body must be maintained through regular exercise and nutrition. Prioritize your bodily health through daily routines. When you have a strong body, you are better positioned to battle adversity and maintain discipline in your life.

- **Mind.** You must bring balance to your thoughts by focusing on positive outlets. Healthy relationships and good time management put you in the best possible frame of mind that creates optimism and reduces stress and mental clutter.

- **Emotions.** Discipline extends to your emotions. Are you able to routinely remain calm, confident, and engaged with the challenges put in front of you? Do your emotions serve you well, or do they drain you? If so, they undermine your ability to implement discipline in your life.

I'm not trying to be funny but using discipline to overcome adversity requires discipline.

When you can combine standards, a commitment to 1% Improvement Days, and the elements of spirit, body, mind, and emotions, you will take big steps in improving your life in many ways.

• • •

- What are the things that block you from being disciplined? What is holding you back from consistently pursuing the goals you have written down? Do you associate with people who inspire, challenge, and invigorate you? Or do you associate with energy and goal vampires who lead you away from the important things in your life?
- How often do you set a goal, fall short, and get discouraged? Do you simply shrug it off and move onto the next goal without examining what went wrong? More importantly, did you ask yourself why you failed? That act alone also requires discipline. Even more important, it requires honesty, which is in short supply for people who make excuses instead of making strides in their life.

Discipline can be the most difficult of all crucibles to master. It requires consistent and directed thought. You must avoid shiny objects and short-term gratification if you ever want to live even a fraction of the life you were meant to live.

Understand that discipline does not happen in a vacuum. You must marry it to standards. For that reason, ask yourself what kind of standards you have in your life. Are they challenging? Are they worthy? Are they appropriate? Do you get energized, even when you understand they might be difficult to achieve and maintain, sometimes for years?

When you master discipline, you have mastered one of the most difficult of all crucibles.

Pay attention to the challenge of discipline and you'll be rewarded handsomely in the end.

The Perspective Crucible

I consider that our present sufferings are not worth comparing with the glory that will be revealed in us.

Romans 8:18

I think a lot about putting things into the proper perspective.

Sometimes it's hard to be honest with yourself when you're locked into your path and your own perspective. Your preconceived ideas can get in the way of reality and make it harder for you to step back from your situation to see things as they truly are.

Can you set aside your pride, your need to always be right, to look at the challenges you face in an unbiased way? That's what you need to do to function at your highest level while building inner trust you can use to base your future actions and decisions.

If you don't, you're only cheating yourself, and ultimately, you're making decisions in the wrong frame of mind. That's a sure path to more difficult challenges and failures down the line.

Perspective requires you to take a step back to fully understand a situation. For example, when you're deep into a Red Zone drive with under two minutes left in the fourth quarter, that's not a good time for perspective.

However, after the game, to improve your performance, you need to take some time and think about how you executed your job. Ask yourself questions and learn how to be brutally honest with yourself. What did you do well? What could you have done better? How could you have been a better teammate? How could you have helped others achieve their peak state when it mattered?

93

Using perspective to your fullest advantage requires acceptance that you're not perfect. You never will be. That there's always room for improvement. That no matter what you do, there will be limitations you'll have to live with and accept.

You'll also need to learn to accept feedback and criticisms from others. In my case, that's what the coaches are for. That's what my teammates are for. We're all feeding into the big goal of winning so it's also important for me to provide my coaches and teammates with real feedback as well. That back-and-forth flow of information is critical on a lot of levels.

The other thing is that perspective, with the right lens, creates growth.

Real positive momentum comes from aligning perspective and acceptance. When you accept perspective, you also accept adversity, but in a way that benefits you. It's like that Jocko Willink video "Good" when he's talking about something going wrong in military combat. No, it's not actually "good" that you get injured, but the mental fight to always find that "good" in adversity is true mental fortitude. That's the perspective that will carry you from good to great.

Perspective impacts the way you prep for a game, mentally and physically. If you deny your perspective, you also deny your ability to get ready for the next big challenge in your life, whether that's taking the field on a Sunday, or in any other challenge you face.

I've also found that perspective makes the game fun. When you're honest with yourself, you cut ties with those things that don't serve you well. You narrow your focus and intensity. You escape stress and anxiety as you become the optimal version of yourself. I guarantee you need every bit of that and then some, every time you step on the field.

Working with optimal perspective and acceptance means you also recover quicker after the fact. Dealing with a targeted set of facts and other honest input means you don't waste time. You study your performance, adjust accordingly, and embrace what comes next, with complete confidence that you're doing the right things for the right reasons. That's how you trust yourself.

When you can trust yourself, you become a force to be reckoned with. You're cultivating an unshakeable foundation based on principles, standards, and facts. This strong foundation allows you to build effective habits that lead to extreme growth.

Employing proper perspective week after week, season after season, and year after year puts you closer to the biggest goals of your life.

On the flip side, if you don't operate this way, you'll become trapped in a limited version of yourself. A nagging frustration will grow inside of you, and you'll lose your mental edge. Losing your mental edge is a big step toward losing your physical edge.

If you're a professional football player, that can spell the end of your career.

Priority and Perspective

It makes no sense to equally devote your thoughts to big things and small things. The big three priorities for me are faith, family, and then football. That decision has been made and will not be impacted, no matter what my current situation is. Perspective requires that you understand the magnitude of a situation and be able to focus on those things that will have the biggest impacts on your life. That is how you can keep those priorities straight and trust that you're accomplishing daily goals that will lead to your ultimate success.

For example, recovering from my ACL injury, the number one priority in football I have right now is doing my exercises and listening to my doctors so that I can heal completely. The most important thing to me, that main goal, is stepping back on that field and playing again. But I can't do that until I make recovery my number one priority right here and right now. When I take that stance, it's easy to put recovery into the proper perspective.

In life, we'd all like to skip ahead of the hard parts and get to the good things. But life doesn't work that way. You must understand the magnitude and the processes to take before you can cross over your own goal lines.

Priorities and perspectives also involve paying attention to the outside world. When I got injured, the Raiders brought in several potential replacements for me. The implications of someone else's decision impacted how I thought daily. Would the replacement take my spot permanently? Did the Raiders not value my services and talents anymore? How would all of this play out?

The magnitude of these questions was huge. They also required that I put them into perspective. All of them had rational answers but until I stepped back, I couldn't see and accept what those answers were.

Your mind plays tricks on you if you let it. The higher the priority in your life, the greater those tricks can be. You can calm those thoughts with proper perspective. Place faith in your efforts, and only control what you can control. The rest you need to let go of, otherwise it will drive you nuts!

Rediscovering Perspective in Marina del Rey

When you're a professional athlete, any injury will mess with your mind as much as your body. When it's something as serious as a torn ACL, everything gets amplified a million times over.

Recovery is a solo journey, no matter how great your support network is. Unless you're a rare breed, you travel to dark places from time to time. I've been there quite a bit over the past several months. You think differently in those types of places, not wrong, just different.

Even if you have faith you'll fully recover physically, you wonder what the ultimate toll will be on you spiritually, mentally, and emotionally.

I had surgery in Los Angeles to repair my ACL by one of the best doctors in the world. Thanks to modern surgical medicine, he left me with a small scar and the pain, even right after the surgery, wasn't all that bad. I caught a break because I had an isolated tear on my ACL. It could have been a lot worse.

After surgery, I had to stay in Los Angeles for a week to start my recovery. The Raiders took great care of me, putting me up in the Ritz Carlton in nearby Marina del Rey, without a doubt, one of the nicest places I've ever stayed.

I couldn't move my knee for a week and with limited mobility, even though my fiancé Alexa and my dad were staying with me, I started to dip into those dark spaces, partly because I'm more down to earth and blue collar than a five-star hotel kind of a guy. I'm into self-parking as opposed to someone who tips the bellhop $20 every time I get out of my car.

Instead of being a place where I could chill, I felt uneasy from the start. My grit and grind mentality immediately started battling the luxury surrounding me.

Rather than go completely stir crazy, I turned my thoughts inward.

Through this adversity, the down time turned into an opportunity to bring added perspective to my life.

I took a deep dive into what was important to me and how I would approach my upcoming rehab. That physical helplessness forced me to think differently. I combined perspective, acceptance, and magnitude in my search for meaning and the truth.

When I combined all those things, I made up my mind to dig deeper than I ever had before and be the standard against all others for my rehab. The rehab was intense, but I'll be honest with you, the most difficult part of that first few weeks was watching the Raiders play the Dallas Cowboys on Thanksgiving Day from my bougie, ritzy, totally uncomfortable hotel room in Marina del Rey.

It only made matters worse when the game went into overtime, and really sucked watching Foster Moreau mess up the coin toss when I told him to call tails pre-game.

Here's a little explanation on the coin toss and a quick insight on just how superstitious football players can be. I was the coin flip guy before getting injured and our team passed that privilege along to Foster. Believe it or not, I had the best coin flip record in the NFL in 2022. And there's a graph somewhere on Twitter to prove it!

As a way of staying connected to the team, Foster would Facetime me before every game and I'd tell him what to call . . . heads or tails. On Thanksgiving Day, Foster lost the first toss in Dallas when I told him to call tails.

Instead of sticking with the initial call in overtime he switched at the last second to heads. Yep, you know what it landed on. There's a video and you can see his big smile because he knew he messed up. I'm just glad we still won the game!

Some people think that being put up in the Ritz Carlton in Marina del Rey would be the vacation of a lifetime. It was just the opposite for me. It was excruciating. Game days, especially on Thanksgiving, put me in a dark place.

I was never happier than the day I flew back to Las Vegas. Armed with my newfound perspective, I started my rehab in earnest. My whole attitude changed once I was around my teammates, training facilities, and all my professional family again.

Marina del Rey was a valuable experience for me. I learned more about who I was at that moment, and who I wanted to be. Although it was uncomfortable, that time was critical in gaining perspective against a backdrop of adversity.

I still had a lot of obstacles to overcome, and I didn't like watching games at home on my couch or from the coach's box for home games, but I was mentally tougher after taking a step back to understand what I had been through, and what was still to come.

That Time the Extension Didn't Happen

The biggest challenge I've ever faced with the Perspective Crucible is the time my contract extension didn't happen.

After my injury and still in the middle of rehabbing, I watched Sutton Smith, a good guy and great fullback, get a two-year extension before I was offered one.

Granted, my injury probably caused management to put my extension on hold. Football is a business. I get that.

That didn't take the sting out of watching Sutton get a new contract. Every player in the league who's gone through something similar will tell you this leads to a sinking feeling in your gut, overthinking, second-guessing, and a little bit of mistrust, especially after you've given everything you have to your team and organization.

It didn't help matters that I was on Twitter quite a bit, watching who got extended and who didn't throughout the league.

I fought through it, and after I was done with all those negative emotions, I went back to what I could control, my rehab process. I went back to help my teammates break down film, put in a lot of time on my nonprofit foundation, and spent quality time with Alexa. These things all helped in different but important ways.

I was further buoyed by the fact that I was healing quickly, ahead of schedule by every measurable metric at my 6- and 12-week marks. Stabilization and strengthening exercises are dull and repetitive, but completely necessary because there's only so much your body can do in a healing process. Even though I could do more intense exercises, protocols are in place to make sure I didn't overextend myself and jeopardize a full recovery. Doing my rehab work in the training facility helped a lot in minimizing the slow and repetitive recovery process.

I kept getting more and more fired up at the prospect of returning to my team at full strength next season.

I kept trusting that I would contractually be taken care of soon enough.

Except that's not what happened.

When I got a chance to sit down with new Raiders management, I was told that even if I recovered fully, there was probably not going to be a place on the team for me next season.

That news flattened me. All my work, accomplishments, and contributions to the team were dashed in a matter of minutes during that meeting.

Another round of adversity stared me in the face.

I'm human so I did what many people would do in that case. I went home and sulked for a couple of days. I'll spare you the details, but it wasn't a good time to be around me.

What pulled me out of it was my faith. I put things into perspective and reminded myself that God has a plan for me and whatever that plan is, I'll be okay. I wasn't going to be a Raider anymore, but I'd recover from that, grateful for the time I spent with the organization and my incredible teammates.

Then I dug deep and got back into my rehab, working from 8 a.m. to noon every day without fail. I started bolstering myself mentally by reading every motivational book I could get my hands on.

I used perspective to chart a path forward, even if I wasn't sure what that path was. I just knew I'd be ready when it revealed itself to me.

As it turns out, I wouldn't have to wait long.

Overtime

For everyone who has, more will be given, and he will have more
than enough. But from the one who does not have, even what he
has will be taken away from him.

Matthew 25:29–30

The best games always seem to go into overtime.

There's more pressure. More drama. And on the biggest stage at the biggest moments are when the best players rise to the top of their game.

Like heat-seeking missiles, the best players always look for those opportunities. I want to be one of those players. I've worked my entire life to be one of those players.

You can't get there by taking the easy way. You must earn your way into those situations. You must overcome adversity and win when you face the crucibles of your own life.

While I was writing this book, my time with the Raiders came to an end. I've already told you how I felt, the uncertainty, the sense of letdown and disappointment, and wondering what the next chapter in my life would bring.

Welcome to Miami

God moves in His speed and time, but I am grateful in my case that He didn't make me wait long to find out. Less than a day after the free-agent signing period started, the Miami Dolphins reached out and signed me to a two-year deal with a big contract bump.

I went from months of unanswered questions about my health and future to a huge moment of clarity and renewed purpose. Pro athletes live on the edge, understanding that the business can be tough to handle and cruel, so when you're given a new set of downs, that feeling is unlike anything else you'll experience . . . except maybe winning a Super Bowl!

The private doubts I had about my career in the NFL exploded into several million insignificant pieces after signing with Miami. Years of fighting to overcome adversity that I've documented in this book suddenly made sense. Paying the price made sense. Every ounce of sweat, strain, and pain associated with my ACL injury and rehab made sense.

And I am forever grateful to the Dolphins for giving me another chance to keep living my dream and my life's purpose.

I am also reminded that all of us are rewarded in God's time and not in our own.

The Climb After the Climb

I don't view my opportunity to play for the Dolphins as an end to a chapter in my life. I view it as a beginning.

I think of it as being at the base of another mountain to climb. Like all of us, I've already climbed so many. I'm also still in the midst of climbing others, such as continuing rehab, training to be the absolute best football player I can, and being the best possible son, soon-to-be husband, and role model for others.

Looking up from the base of this new mountain, I don't know how tall it is, what obstacles I'll face on the climb, or what emotions I'll have to work through. I just know I'm equipped and ready to show a new organization and set of teammates that I will apply all the lessons I've learned about commitment, grit, determination, and more, to prove that I'm the best teammate these guys have ever seen.

I'm telling you this because I want you to approach your mountains with the highest possible confidence levels when you're still standing at the base.

Sure, it would be easy to let my thoughts drift back to a group of guys I already know on the Raiders in a Las Vegas training facility where everything is familiar. But other than a fleeting thought or two, I need to focus on the future. Every player in the NFL is climbing his own mountains, and if he spends too much time thinking about the past or things that don't serve him well, he stumbles and falls off those mountains, and he'll end up riding the bench or worse, out of the league.

I'm not ready to let that happen to me. I have unfinished business.

I must prove I can climb this mountain.

It is not the mountain I thought I would ever climb, nor were any of the other crucibles I've faced in my life.

But those were God's plans for me.

I understand now that any disappointments I've faced are also part of that plan. They were put in my life as important lessons I can now draw upon, when the mountain is taller and the climb is more challenging.

This climb will not be perfect. Attempting perfection only leads to an unfulfilling journey. Nothing illustrates that point more than one of the first things I learned when I landed in Miami.

Those of you who have followed football for a while are well aware of the accomplishments of the 1972 Dolphins team. Under Coach Don Shula, that team went 14-0 in the regular season and 3-0 in the playoffs for a "perfect" 17-0 season.

Perfect!

Or simply undefeated?

There is a difference.

I guarantee you those players didn't have perfect games. In fact, it's a sure bet they screwed up a lot of times. Coach Shula didn't call perfect plays on every snap. I've been in the locker room, and even after the best games, there are always ways to get better, to make that climb more efficient.

The climb is not about perfection. It's about being the best you can be. It's about relentlessly chasing greatness, personally and as part of a team. It's about supporting your teammates and leaving nothing in reserve that you may never otherwise use.

When you get to the top of the mountain, you want to look back down and know you've earned it. You want to remain humble but confident in knowing that you can climb many other mountains if you can successfully climb this one.

Embrace Your Crucibles

That's what The Seven Crucibles have taught me. I hope they have given you some critical insights as well.

Embrace your crucibles. They have been put in your life for a reason. How you resolve your crucibles forms the foundation of your life.

Focus on your priorities and processes instead of the results. Internalize the climb and learn to love the details.

Create positive friction and use it as a catalyst for growth and change. Look in the mirror and get comfortable with being uncomfortable.

Find peace in your relationships with others, especially in your relationship with God. Be a good human being by being accountable, not selectively, but consistently.

No one cares as much about your life as you do, so go all in despite criticisms from others. In fact, when it makes sense, shut out the useless critics in your life.

Doing these things has allowed me to create the best version of myself as a believer, worshiper, husband, son, teammate, and more.

When you overcome your crucibles, you inspire belief in yourself and how the world sees you.

That's not an easy path at times, but absolutely worth it.

Acknowledgments

I think it's safe to say I'm a football player, not an author. I did my best to bring my story to life through this book, but it really did take a team to share this message with you. It is an ongoing blessing to do my best to inspire others, and I want to take this time to thank everyone who inspires me.

A big thanks has to go out to my family, first and foremost. Alexa, thank you for sticking by my side through this football journey both on and off the field. I am blessed to watch you tackle everything that comes your way.

A special thank you to my little sister Sydnie. Stay on your grind like I know you will; I'm excited to watch your future unfold and so proud to be your big brother.

To my parents, Pat and Chris Ingold, thank you for everything. I'm so grateful for the lessons you taught me along the way and the decisions you helped guide me through. You've laid a heckuva blueprint on how to be great parents and inspire your kids—thank you.

On the football field and in locker rooms, I've been with some of the best life teachers there are. To all my teammates and coaches, thank you for coming to work every day with the respect and commitment to come together as a team.

The team that put this book together was nothing short of excellent.

Bret Colson, thank you for your consistent communication throughout one of the craziest seasons of my life. Your ability to find a way to get all these ideas ironed out and edited throughout all of the "exciting chaos" was inspiring. I'm grateful to have met and worked together on this piece.

Dr. Barbara Lash, Michael Lumpkin, Ben Newman, Jon Gordon, and the IKE homies, thank you all for the feedback and input. Your opinions and advice shaped the way this book reads, and I'm forever grateful for our conversations and relationships that will impact others.

About the Author

Alec Ingold is a National Football League player, founder of the Ingold Family Foundation, and owner of Ingold Companies LLC.

Alec has overcome considerable adversity to realize his dream of playing in the NFL. After going undrafted in 2019, he was named the Las Vegas Raiders' team captain and a Pro Bowl alternate. Alec was also a Walter Payton Man of the Year nominee in 2020, considered the highest honor in all of football, for his work in underserved communities. He eventually became the second-highest paid fullback in the NFL as a Miami Dolphin in 2022.

Alec founded the Ingold Family Foundation to support and draw attention to the adoption and foster care system. He also carries that mission forward by teaching youth financial literacy and professional development skills.

Ingold Companies LLC is part of Alec's continuing community outreach efforts to "Inspire Belief" by motivating others to believe in themselves. He speaks at schools, businesses, and charitable organizations across the country, sharing stories about the challenges he's faced to encourage others to overcome adversity in their lives as well.

Index

115